This Book Will
Make You Confident

Dr Jessamy Hibberd
and
Jo Usmar

Quercus

Quercus Editions Ltd
55 Baker Street
7th Floor, South Block
London
W1U 8EW

First published in 2014

A CIP catalogue record for this book is available from the British Library

ISBN 978 1 84866 285 8
Printed in Great Britain by Clays Ltd, St Ives Plc

10 9 8 7 6 5 4 3 2 1

Designed for Quercus Editions Ltd by Peggy Sadler at Bookworx
www.bookworx.biz

Contents

A note from the authors

We live in ever-changing times and sometimes life can be tough. We're constantly being pulled in different directions and can struggle to cope with the pressure that we're put under by external factors and, most importantly, by ourselves. With greater choice comes greater responsibility and occasionally this can be a breeding ground for stress, unhappiness and self-doubt. There are very few people (if any at all) who feel they operate perfectly in their work, relationships and life in general. Most of us could use some help now and then – a nudge to show us how to improve our mood, to change our approach to life and to feel more content.

This series aims to help you understand why you feel, think and behave the way you do – and then gives you the tools to make positive changes. We're not fans of complicated medical jargon so we've tried to make everything accessible, relevant and entertaining as we know you'll want to see improvements as soon as possible. These concise, practical guides show you how to focus your thinking, develop coping strategies and learn practical techniques to face anything and everything in more positive and helpful ways.

We believe self-help doesn't have to be confusing, worthy or patronising. We draw on our professional experience and the latest research, using anecdotes and examples which we found helpful and hope you will too. Titles are split into particular areas of concern such as sleep problems, unhappiness, a lack of confidence and stress, so you can focus on the areas you'd most like to address.

Our books are based on a Cognitive Behavioural Therapy (CBT)

framework. CBT is an incredibly successful treatment for a wide variety
of issues and we're convinced it will enable you to cope with whatever
you're facing.

Within the books you'll regularly come across diagrams called
mind maps. They are easy to use and simple to understand. Based on
CBT, mind maps show how your thoughts, behaviour and how you
feel (both emotionally and physically) are all connected, breaking
the problem down so it doesn't seem overwhelming, and laying out
options for making changes.

There are exercises and checklists throughout, to guide you through
the practical steps of altering how you feel. We'll make it easy to make
these changes part of your routine because reading the theory is only
going to get you so far. The only way to ensure you'll feel better long-
term is to put everything you learn into practice and change how you
experience your day-to-day life.

You can *choose* to feel better and these books will show you how.

Good luck! Let us know how you get on by contacting us on our
website: www.jessamyandjo.com

Jessamy and Jo

Introduction

The *Oxford English Dictionary* defines confidence as 'a feeling of self-assurance arising from an appreciation of one's own abilities or qualities'. What it doesn't add is that a lack of confidence can affect your whole life, making absolutely everything seem harder, gloomier and less achievable. That's not just hyperbole – it's absolutely true. Confidence is intrinsically tangled up with how you judge your ability to cope with whatever life throws at you. It's all about self-esteem – how you measure your own self-worth and value. If you believe you're lacking in any way your outlook about everything can be tinged with grey, leading to a tendency to feel anxious, stressed and even depressed. You'll devalue your achievements and alter your goals and ambitions to reflect your insecurity.

While this all sounds pretty dark don't worry, there's good news too.

First up, you can feel more confident and increase your self-esteem. There are simple strategies within this book that will teach you how to appreciate the skills and qualities that you have. It doesn't matter how entrenched your negative belief system is, if you're really determined to feel better you can reconstruct it to reflect a much more positive and realistic impression of yourself.

Secondly, lacking confidence occasionally is totally normal. It's a natural response to all manner of events, thoughts, beliefs or demands placed upon you by others and that you place upon yourself. Everyone's different and how people deal with insecurity will vary hugely, but human beings are designed to experience the full spectrum of emotions – everything from over-confidence bordering on egotism to crippling self-doubt. You'll inevitably slide up and down this scale depending on what's going on in your life, but ideally you'll rest somewhere in the middle for the majority of the time. However, problems start when you've been stuck down the self-doubt end for ages and self-belief is a distant memory.

Why choose this book?

It can be all too easy to accept a lack of confidence and low self-esteem as permanent fixtures in your life, but that's a terrible plan. Believing that you're not clever enough, witty enough, attractive enough, ambitious enough or generally just good enough can be intensely debilitating. We're confident that 'This Book Will Make You Confident' whether you suffer from occasional bouts of insecurity to a full-blown 24/7 desire to hide away.

We've both fallen into confidence black holes at various points in our lives and would have loved to have a book such as this on hand to deliver a dose of reassurance and courage. When you start questioning yourself you can lose all sense of rationality and perspective. This book will explain why you feel the way you do, how your behaviour might be contributing and maintaining these feelings, how negative thoughts are pesky buggers and why your body might react in certain ways. You'll then be given the tools to change these things for the better.

We want to give practical and helpful advice in a simple and entertaining way, minus any speculative airy-fairy nonsense. What we're recommending is proven to work and it will help you.

How it all works

This is a manual on how to feel more confident and increase your self-esteem. This means you're actually going to have to try out the strategies and techniques within to see any benefits. Investing time and energy into this will change your life.

As previously mentioned, we'll be using Cognitive Behavioural Therapy throughout this book, which is explained in more detail in Chapter 2. It's a highly effective problem-focused approach that finds simple and practical ways of managing the here and now. It will give you a set of tools to help you change how you view yourself and what's happening around you, giving you the confidence in your abilities that's sorely lacking. These tools will last forever – there's no time limit on what you'll learn – so whenever you find yourself thinking, 'I'm not good enough,' or 'I can't do this,' you'll be able to use them to step back and take a far more realistic view of what's going on.

How to get the most out of this book

+ Read the chapters in numerical order as each one builds on the last.
+ Try all of the strategies out, rather than just skipping through them. (The strategies are all identified by Ⓢ.) We're not suggesting them as part of some shady experiment – they're proven to work. Some may suit you better than others, but by trying them all you'll be giving yourself the best chance of boosting your confidence long-term.
+ Practice. Some of what we recommend might be quite tough or totally alien to you – the more you practise the easier it will get and

the sooner it will become second nature. You have got into the habit of putting yourself down and breaking bad habits can take time. While some of these strategies will have immediate results, others might take longer to get the hang of. Don't be discouraged, just keep at it and you will see results.

+ Buy a new notebook to dedicate specifically to this book. We'll be asking you to scribble things down and draw things out, which is a really important part of the process. Writing things down aids memory and will make your determination to change more 'official' in your head. Also, it'll be really motivational to flick back through and see how far you've come.

You don't have to let a lack of confidence inhibit you, make you feel you're not up to scratch or alter what you want to do in life. You absolutely can increase your self-esteem and feel good about yourself no matter what's happened to you in the past or how long you've been feeling insecure. Just picking up this book and thinking about taking charge of your confidence issues should already make you feel stronger! That's a huge step and things will only get better from there.

1

In Strict Confidence

Insecurity and low self-esteem can act as terrible twins, wreaking havoc in your head and causing untold damage to your life. Here we explain what they are and why they might have got their claws into you.

What are confidence and self-esteem?

On a very basic level, confidence is a feeling of emotional security that comes from having faith in yourself and self-esteem is an umbrella term incorporating everything that makes up that faith. Confidence is built from several factors, of which self-esteem is one of the most important.

Feeling confident is essential in all aspects of your life. It helps you to reach your goals, to try new things, to believe in your decision-making capabilities and to be independent. It enables you to manage stress and equips you to deal with emotional, practical and physical problems. It's how you measure your ability to cope and to succeed, so a lack of confidence can be exceptionally debilitating, making you feel you don't measure up in some way.

Don't get us wrong, feeling confident doesn't equate to never feeling nervous, anxious or uncertain. Anxiety and uncertainty are normal human emotions and everyone will experience them in their lifetime – yep, even megalomaniacs feel under pressure sometimes. Confidence varies according to what you're doing, what you're facing, your age, your experience, the context and your mood. However, you're much more likely to only face occasional blips in confidence if your self-esteem is generally pretty high, you're a positive person and you trust yourself to cope with difficult situations.

Please note though that confidence is not the same as arrogance – that's a whole different kettle of fish. Arrogance is an overbearing pride, a superiority complex that is in no way realistic or helpful, while true confidence is an inner strength based upon self-respect.

You can fake confidence, of course, by pretending to be something you're not or by putting on an act, but unless it's an exceptionally

What makes us confident?

+ **Self-esteem**, which is self-respect and faith in yourself built upon:
  Self-assurance: believing in the validity of your opinions and beliefs
  Self-acceptance: knowing who you are, what you like and what you dislike
  Self-belief: knowing you can achieve what you set out to
+ Feeling 'authentic' and comfortable in your own skin
+ Being at ease with yourself physically
+ Having a positive attitude and approach to life
+ Having faith in your ability to tackle difficult, risky or uncertain situations
+ A willingness to accept both praise and criticism, without it radically changing how you feel about yourself

accomplished act then usually you're just flagging up how uncertain of yourself you really are. No one feels confident all the time and feeling stressed, anxious or worried should in no way be considered a weakness.

Fearing your ability to cope can become a self-fulfilling prophecy. You feel less confident, worry about your capabilities and so you start behaving out of character or in unhelpful ways which, more often than not, will actually inhibit you from succeeding. When you don't achieve what you set out to, this then proves your original fears about not being up to the job, causing your confidence to plummet even further. It's exactly what happened to Steven. He was frightened of

Example: Steven's swagger

Steven had just started his new job as regional sales manager of a large company. He was in charge of a staff of thirty and felt completely out of his depth. Many of the people he was supposed to be managing were older and more experienced than him. He thought the best way to handle his unease was to completely disguise it. On his first day he strutted into the office, called a meeting, introduced himself, cracked a few jokes, dismissed everyone and sauntered off. He was so frightened that people might suspect he didn't know what he was doing that he didn't ask any questions or seek guidance on anything. If he didn't know the process for something he just did it a different way.

Where he thought he was coming across as capable, efficient and chatty, his staff actually found him boorish, arrogant and disrespectful. They knew he was too proud to ask for help so they didn't offer any and things quickly went from bad to worse.

being considered inexperienced and he ended up behaving in a way that ensured he would be thought inexperienced. It's a vicious circle – see opposite.

Low self-esteem (LSE)

Low self-esteem plays such a big role in confidence that it gets its own acronym: LSE. Having low self-esteem is caused by not believing

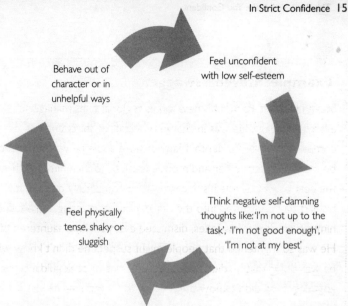

Feel unconfident
with low self-esteem

Think negative self-damning
thoughts like: 'I'm not up to the
task', 'I'm not good enough',
'I'm not at my best'

Feel physically
tense, shaky or
sluggish

Behave out of
character or in
unhelpful ways

yourself up to the task, not trusting your instincts and not believing you're worth it. You assume things won't work out, you criticise and blame yourself and engage in unhelpful behaviours (such as avoidance, procrastination, comfort eating, being defensive, etc.). This only exacerbates the problem and confirms your negative beliefs. Events, situations or even just thoughts can provoke LSE, but once it's got its claws into you it can go viral, spreading fast and influencing other parts of your life that were previously fine.

What causes low confidence and LSE?

A lack of confidence or LSE can be specific to certain situations (as in the case of Steven) or they can become permanent fixtures in your life that affect everything. If you're feeling insecure about a particular event or situation you can still have a positive perspective of yourself in general. Your confidence issues will then disappear once you feel the issue is resolved. For example, you might be feeling very unconfident about meeting a specific deadline. You don't believe you're up to it and so you avoid starting the project. You inevitably do miss the deadline, but it's not the end of the world, as you're given an extension. Your confidence increases as soon as the situation is resolved and this dip in self-esteem won't have affected any other part of your life.

However, if low confidence and LSE are permanent fixtures they can colour everything you do, say, think or feel. Thoughts of being stupid, ugly, useless, not good enough, worthless, unattractive, unlovable and a failure, will rear their head in difficult situations or all the time.

These beliefs tend to be deep-rooted and you see them as facts rather than just opinions you hold about yourself. You'll believe that they are fundamental features of your identity and who you are, which unsurprisingly often means you don't like yourself all that much.

People become unconfident and develop LSE as a result of negative experiences in their lives that often have their roots in childhood or adolescence; however it can develop at any time. Even people with previously healthy self-esteem and bucket-loads of confidence can have it chipped away in later life if they go through a stressful experience that changes how they view themselves, e.g. hating their job, falling out with a friend or being in a destructive relationship. It can even be caused by a change of role that wouldn't necessarily be considered negative, i.e. becoming a parent, retiring, or having your kids leave home. These kinds of events and situations alter your place in the world and take you out of your comfort zone. This can cause an identity crisis which will have a big effect on confidence levels.

Example: Megan's identity crisis

Megan had been single for years. She'd always thought she would love to settle down and had started feeling anxious as more of her friends paired off. She was often the token single girl at gatherings where everyone always tried to set her up with totally unsuitable men and she'd end up feeling like Bridget Jones.

Then she met Phil. Funny, charismatic and attractive, she thought she'd found her perfect match and the relationship moved quickly. They moved in together within four months. And then things went wrong.

Megan had never lived with anyone before, while Phil had lived with his ex for six years. She felt unprepared for her new role as a 'live-in girlfriend'. She didn't know what was expected of her, how she was meant to act and whether she was allowed to just eat beans on toast for dinner whenever she felt like it as she used to. She wasn't used to taking someone else's routine into consideration and felt guilty when she didn't run stuff past him, but also slightly resentful that she had to. And it's not like Phil was demanding in anyway, he was really laid-back.

Megan went from being laid-back and confident to feeling as if she was letting both Phil and herself down – and she didn't know how or why.

Nature versus nurture

Your experiences influence how you see yourself, how valued you feel by others and how much you value yourself. As a child you learn from what you see, hear and what you're told. You don't have the same means to question things when you're a kid as you do when you're an adult so you generally accept what you're told as fact because you have no basis for comparison. This is unfortunately where a lot of problems can start.

If you were told you were useless or were never praised or rewarded for your achievements in your youth you're far more likely to suffer from LSE as an adult and its likely to be more severe and harder to shift. This is because you've never had a chance to see yourself positively (unlike if it develops in adulthood). If you've never had a chance to build confidence you have nothing to fall back on in difficult times – there's no positive self-belief system to help you out. You'll automatically think you're not good enough, attractive enough, clever enough, etc. as you've never had an alternative view.

However, if you were loved, praised and supported as a child you're more likely to have healthy self-esteem and be pretty confident now. Having experienced feeling confident, loved and capable you'll find it easier to recall those emotions when you go through harder times.

So that's the nurture side, but nature plays a big role too. Your genetic inheritance from your parents contributes to your temperament which can influence how likely you are to feel confident or to suffer from LSE. If you are an extrovert, you'll enjoy taking risks and will be happy to leave your comfort zone to see what you're capable of and put your skills to the test. Extroverts usually have and exhibit a healthy self-esteem. On the other hand, if you're an introvert you're more likely to hang back, stay quiet and keep things safe meaning you'll rarely get the chance to have your opinions validated or to see that you can cope with challenging situations. Introverts are usually more susceptible to LSE. There is a middle ground of course, but whatever traits you were born with will be either curtailed or emphasised by how you're bought up.

Ideas about confidence and self-esteem developed in childhood can be tricky to change as they've become part of your internal belief system, shaping how you interpret events and view yourself in adulthood.

However, as mentioned above, even if you were a really confident kid you can still suffer from self-esteem and confidence issues as you get older. Below we've listed some common confidence killers that can fundamentally change how you view yourself.

Common confidence killers

The severity with which the experiences below might affect you depends on how often they happen, how much you believe them at the time and how long they last. They can be happening right now or have happened to you while you were growing up.

+ Feeling you can't cope with stress: Believing that you can't handle a current event or situation can make you feel discouraged, demoralised and lonely. This will undermine your confidence and you can develop LSE. Examples include: being bullied or intimidated at work, being in an abusive relationship, going through a break-up, feeling isolated from friends or family, going through a life change (i.e. becoming a parent or being made redundant), financial hardship, uncertainty about the future, experiencing a traumatic event or health problems (your own or those of someone close to you).

+ Not meeting standards: This can be two-fold – you don't feel you're meeting the standards others expect of you and you expect of yourself. You may know you're not performing well or it may be openly acknowledged by others and you can be criticised (see below), dismissed or made fun of.

+ Constant criticism: Being able to accept constructive criticism is an integral part of being a functioning adult, but when the criticism is unwarranted, severe or constant and is never balanced by praise and acknowledgment of your successes it can shatter your confidence and self-esteem. How much criticism affects you will also be determined by who's dishing it out and how much you value their opinion (i.e. if it's your boss, the office intern, your friend, your parent or your partner).

+ Absence of positives: No one is overtly horrible to you, but there's a distinct lack of attention, praise, encouragement, time, warmth and affection lavished on you. No one seems that interested in you personally. As a child you will conclude that this is because there's something wrong with you and you don't deserve it, but these feelings can be triggered or re-triggered in adulthood too.

+ Feeling like an outcast: You feel (or felt when you were a kid) like the odd one out either at school, home, work or in general. Although you might not be criticised for your 'different' interests, abilities or personality you feel they are negatively emphasised, while your peers' attributes are praised or celebrated. Popular culture can play a big role in deciding whether you believe you're 'normal' or not, especially when it comes to physical appearance, social interests and popularity.

+ Family problems: Divorce, illness or job loss can hugely affect families – how they interact and whether they offer the stability they used to or they're expected to. Also your role within a family – how you are viewed and represented within the dynamic – can play a big part in how you view yourself and how you think others view you. You might feel unable to update the character you believe you were assigned a long time ago (i.e. the black sheep, the clever one, the unreliable one, etc.)

+ Your social position: How you view yourself is heavily influenced by how you believe you fit into society. Class, wealth, ethnicity, political views and religion all shape how we see ourselves and our families. Experiencing prejudice or hostility based on someone's conviction that you or your views are somehow 'unacceptable' can dramatically affect your judgements of self-worth.

+ Abuse (physical, emotional or sexual): If you suffered abuse, were frequently punished, neglected or mistreated as a child, this will have left its scars. Children often interpret the things that happen to them as their responsibility – that it is in some way their fault – which can have lasting implications for self-esteem. Being subjected to abuse in adulthood can be just as damaging as the self-blame cycle is still present. You may believe that as an adult you should be able to do something about it or that because you made certain choices you have to live with them. This isn't true. Whether you were abused as a child or an adult it was absolutely not your fault

– it should never have happened and you are 100 per cent not responsible for it.

The impact of low confidence and LSE

The impact of feeling you don't quite measure up or are lacking in some way can be absolutely catastrophic. And how you feel and think will inevitably affect what you do. Below are some typical behavioural responses to feeling insecure:

✦ Become introverted or an extrovert: If you feel self-conscious and become over-sensitive to criticism or disapproval you might either shy away from social interaction or court it, becoming a people-pleaser.

✦ Become a workaholic or workshy: A fear of failure or feeling like a fraud can either make you work non-stop and try to prove yourself or make you avoid work altogether so if you fail you can use your lack of effort as an excuse.

✦ Ignore compliments and praise: You'll focus only on the negatives, undermining your ability and role, ignoring anything that suggests you're actually coping or doing well.

Help for past traumas

Victims of childhood and adult trauma can and do recover. Seeking professional advice from a specialist in trauma or abuse can help you to work through what has happened. You can visit your GP if you are interested in seeking further help and they can direct you to the relevant specialist.

+ Avoid and procrastinate: You'll run away from or put off facing anything where you'll be judged or evaluated or that might cause conflict (i.e. a work project or a messy break-up). You also won't try new things in case you struggle at them (which would be totally normal!).

+ Don't look after yourself: The lack of value you place on yourself means you don't see much point in caring about your appearance or health. You might over- or under-eat, stop exercising, self-medicate with alcohol or drugs and ignore your personal hygiene. Or you might do totally the opposite and over-exercise and spend hours perfecting your appearance based on a supposition of what is attractive.

Confidence can be learned, so wherever your insecurity has come from it doesn't have to rule your life.

Thoughts to take away

✓ You *can* stop the vicious circle of LSE by changing how you feel, think and act

✓ It doesn't matter whether your confidence problems and LSE started as a kid or as an adult – there are proactive things you can do to fix them

✓ Feeling insecure sometimes is totally normal – you just have to learn how to ensure that it is only *sometimes*

2

Cognitive Behavioural Therapy and Confidence

Cognitive Behavioural Therapy (CBT) is a brilliant way of dealing with all your confidence and LSE issues. Here we explain what it is and how it will help you personally.

What is CBT?

Cognitive Behavioural Therapy may sound like it involves trying to summon electricity through tin-foil hats, but thankfully that couldn't be further from the truth. CBT is one of the leading problem-focused treatments for a broad variety of disorders including depression, anxiety, insomnia and yes, low self-esteem. Pioneered by Dr Aaron T. Beck in the 1960s and recommended by the National Institute of Clinical Excellence (NICE), CBT gives you back control of how you feel, think and behave by teaching you practical strategies to deal with whatever's happening in your life and to manage your emotional health.

CBT has been proven to increase self-esteem and is well established as a treatment for both anxiety and depression (both key factors in

Example: Emma's embarrassment

Emma recognised an old friend, Tom, in a restaurant. Surprised and pleased, she walked over and said hello. 'Um, hi?' he replied. It was obvious he had no idea who she was. Rather than introduce herself, Emma stuttered and stumbled over her words and quickly shuffled off, feeling mortified. Thoughts like, 'Can I really be that forgettable?' ran through her head which had a domino effect, causing her body to tense up and her heart to start beating rapidly. She returned to her table, sitting quietly and appearing distracted for the rest of the evening. She was too embarrassed to explain to her companion what had happened.

triggering and maintaining LSE).

The fundamental basis of CBT is that the way we think about ourselves will influence how we feel emotionally and physically and how we behave. And, how we think about ourselves is triggered by how we interpret situations, i.e. it's not what happens that affects us, it's how we evaluate what happens.

Emma's negative interpretation of this event left her feeling insecure emotionally and riled up physically. It also prompted her to behave out of character (by being quiet throughout dinner) which aggravated her feelings of LSE as she then started worrying and feeling guilty about ruining her friend's night out.

What happened to Emma can be illustrated in a nifty diagram called a mind map, see page 28.

If Emma had been feeling more confident and hadn't been suffering from LSE she no doubt would have interpreted the event differently. It had been five years since they last saw each other, perhaps Tom just didn't recognise her with her new haircut? By thinking about things more realistically (did Tom have any reason to be deliberately rude or is it far more likely he was just taken unawares?) she could have introduced herself and reminded him of their past acquaintance. No doubt he would have remembered her and they would have had a chat. This would have made her feel better physically and emotionally and she would have returned to her table feeling good.

Your behaviour, physicality and thoughts can all act as intervention points. If you change one it will have a knock-on effect on all the others, including your mood. For example, if Emma had changed her behaviour and instead of being quiet throughout dinner had explained

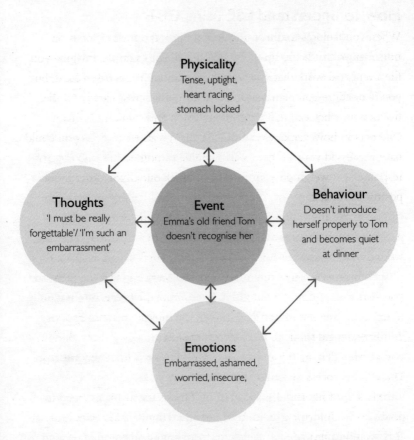

what happened to her friend so they could laugh about it together, she would have felt better physically and emotionally and her thoughts would have been more positive. CBT teaches you how all of these things interlink so you can choose how you want to feel, act and think.

How to understand LSE using CBT

When you feel low and insecure you are programmed to focus on information that backs up the way you feel. For example, imagine you file a report at work that you're uncertain about. You worked hard, but you're not sure you managed to get your point across clearly. Of the five people who read it, four of them love it and think it's brilliant. One person however, doesn't think it's that great. He reckons you could have expressed yourself better on a couple of points. This one negative response will weigh on your mind and block out all the other more positive feedback.

To manage the volume of information that you encounter day-to-day, your brain chooses what to flag up to your consciousness and it will actively look for proof to validate your beliefs. You don't have time or space to run through the nitty gritty of everything that happens, so you start to do things on autopilot. For example, when you're learning to drive and see a stop sign you look in the mirror and start braking. You prepare and think about the steps of slowing down. But, after you've been driving for a few years you'll see a red light and just stop. The whole process becomes automatic.

This way of filtering information enables us to live at the frenetic pace we do. Unfortunately though, negative thought processes can also become automatic. If you suffer from confidence problems your brain will have become tuned to automatically pay attention to the bad things that are consistent with your negative view of yourself.

When processing goes wrong ...

The negative biases your brain harbours as a result of LSE keep your confidence levels low. You expect things to reflect badly on you or to turn out negatively and so you actively contribute to them through how you think and act. In situations where you feel nervous or unsure of yourself your negative beliefs come into force and you'll only pay attention to anything that confirms them (i.e. 'They're laughing at me', or 'They don't think I'm good enough').

You've become a master at identifying the tiniest mistakes you make and will dwell on your perceived shortcomings and flaws, screening out anything good about yourself until you can no longer recognise your strengths and qualities. Instead of seeing mistakes and weaknesses as part of being human and an essential part of learning, you view it as evidence of your inadequacy and your inability to cope.

Picture a kid's shape-sorter toy, where the spheres go in the round holes and the cubes into the square holes. When you have LSE your brain turns into one of these toys and will only accept any positive information that fits exceptionally strict parameters. The info has to be the right size and shape before you'll acknowledge it. However, as soon as it comes to negative information your brain ditches the shape-sorter and welcomes it all with open arms.

How negative biases affect you

As already illustrated in Emma's mind map, how you interpret an event will affect how you think, feel emotionally and physically, and how you act. If you're overly self-critical and are plagued with self-doubt this will prompt you to behave in ways that exacerbate these feelings.

You'll be more likely to avoid starting long-term projects or to quit them when they become difficult. These behaviours lead to or maintain negative emotions e.g. anxiety, low mood, frustration, shame and guilt. Also, anxiety and fear will trigger your inbred fight or flight reflex which will make your body tense up, your heart race, your breathing go crazy and your blood flood to your extremities. This extreme physical reaction is great if you're stuck in a lion's enclosure at the local zoo, but not so great if you're meeting your in-laws.

Ⓢ Symptom checklist

Below are some common ways of thinking, behaving and feeling emotionally and physically that are triggered by low confidence and LSE. Tick off the ones that apply to you. Starting to think about how LSE affects you personally will show you how all of your reactions are related and how they're all contributing to the problem.

Thoughts

❑ Self-doubt: questioning the choices you've made and your ability to make them in the future

❑ Self-criticism: beating yourself up for your mistakes and focusing on your 'failures', i.e. 'I deserve this because I'm not good enough'

❑ Blaming yourself when things go wrong even if they weren't your fault or responsibility

❑ Focusing on things you view as your weaknesses and flaws

- ❏ Discounting anything positive, i.e. 'That doesn't count because…'
- ❏ Always expecting the worst, i.e. 'This is never going to work' or 'I can't cope with the repercussions'
- ❏ Constantly comparing yourself negatively to others
- ❏ Believing you are out of your depth or unprepared

Behaviour

- ❏ Self-deprecating jokes
- ❏ Putting yourself down (not in a jokey way)
- ❏ Explaining away compliments, i.e. 'It was luck', 'It's not a big deal', 'anyone could have done it'
- ❏ Difficulty speaking out or asserting yourself
- ❏ Overly apologetic
- ❏ Avoiding challenges and new opportunities
- ❏ Aggressive
- ❏ Perfectionist
- ❏ Reacting badly to criticism or disapproval
- ❏ Don't give praise or compliments to others
- ❏ Shy or self-conscious
- ❏ Avoiding socialising
- ❏ Changing your speech e.g. speaking more quietly, quickly, fumbling your words or changing pitch

Emotions

☐ Sad
☐ Depressed
☐ Guilty
☐ Ashamed
☐ Anxious
☐ Embarrassed
☐ Frustrated
☐ Doubtful/
☐ Angry
Uncertain

Physicality

☐ Tense
☐ Fidgety
☐ Tired
☐ Poor posture, i.e. hunched
☐ Sluggish
over
☐ Increased heart rate
☐ Defensive stance i.e.
☐ Demotivated
crossed arms
☐ Distracted

Example: Fred's fraud fears

Fred felt like a fraud. He always presented himself as cheerful, funny and charismatic, but was also forthright in his opinions and stood his ground. His friends constantly said, 'You're so sure of yourself,' and he'd laugh, but inwardly panic. The trouble ⋯⋯

⋯⋯⋯⋯> was he really believed it was an act. Inside he was riddled with insecurity. He only ever seemed confident in his opinions because he made sure he said them in a determined way – a trick he learned from his dad. He was actually terrified of being challenged in case he couldn't back up what he'd said.

He believed everyone had fallen for his performance and he could be exposed any second. He couldn't show any insecurity or he'd shatter the carefully constructed illusion he'd created. He constantly felt like he was tiptoeing along a high-wire. If people liked this version of him didn't that prove that the 'real' version who suffered from self-doubt wasn't good enough?

Fred's fears are completely unjustified. First up, how good an actor can he be? If he appears confident, funny and in control then that's because he is. You can't fake charisma full-time! Also, he needs to remember that everyone suffers from insecurity and asking for help when you need it is not a sign of weakness, it's actually very brave. People might even find it strange that he doesn't ever seem to suffer from the same worries they do.

❺ Your own mind map

We'd like you to fill in your own mind map. Focus on a recent event that made you feel insecure in some way. Perhaps you felt you didn't look good enough, didn't finish something adequately, embarrassed

Fred's mind map looks
like this:

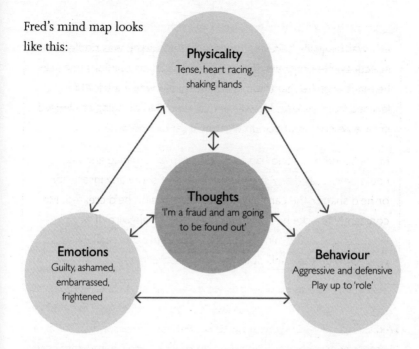

Physicality
Tense, heart racing,
shaking hands

Thoughts
'I'm a fraud and am going
to be found out'

Emotions
Guilty, ashamed,
embarrassed,
frightened

Behaviour
Aggressive and defensive
Play up to 'role'

yourself or didn't give your opinion when it mattered. Write it down.
Try to remember how it made you feel emotionally, physically, what
it made you think and what it led you to do or want to do. Flick back
to the tick list of symptoms to jog your memory if necessary and use
both Emma's and Fred's experiences as guides.

Thinking deeply about a specific event will allow you to see how
low confidence and LSE affect you personally. You may believe the
thought, 'My boss always criticises me because I'm not good enough,'
is a totally justified fact that summarises the situation perfectly and that
doesn't have any lasting implications on your feelings of self-worth –

but you'd be wrong. So wrong. That one thought will make you feel low emotionally and either sluggish or riled up physically, which will then influence your behaviour.

Note down which part of the mind map you found easiest to fill out. You might experience LSE very physically and constantly feel like you've got a brick sitting in your stomach. Or you might be criticised and ignore the person and this behaviour will then trigger feelings of guilt and embarrassment which influence your negative thoughts. Whatever you remembered first is your jumping off point and from there you can fill in the gaps.

The better you get at identifying all four parts the more tools you'll have later on for making changes and feeling more confident. We'll be introducing strategies to help you do this throughout the book. Using Fred's mind map as an example, we have suggested some of the sorts of things you should be asking and telling yourself when you feel this way:

Thoughts: If you're really a fraud you must be an exceptionally good one to have maintained this 'character' for so long. You can't fake being funny or charismatic. What do you mean by 'being found out'? If you're defining that as exhibiting some insecurities then that's ridiculous as everyone feels insecure sometimes – even generally positive and confident people. No one will think any less of you for exhibiting self-doubt, in fact they'll probably respect you for asking for help.
Physical response: Your body is reacting to your fear and alerting you to the fact that there's a situation that needs dealing with. Behaving as if you're under threat (i.e. by withdrawing, becoming aggressive, fidgety or introverted) will produce the same physical and emotional response

as if you really were in danger. If you act in a calm and neutral way it will keep your thoughts, emotions and physical responses in check.
Behaviour: Being defensive and aggressive only flags up your insecurity, as you'll seem unsure of yourself and unwilling to accept other people's opinions. It's important to keep doing things that you find challenging so you can learn, improve and convince yourself that you can do it. This will increase your confidence.

Challenging any of the above points will have a domino effect on the others and will lift your mood. If Fred followed those tips his new mind map would look like this:

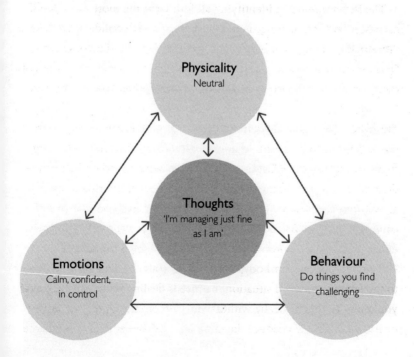

⑤ Thoughts aren't facts

This is a key aspect of CBT and a great philosophy to remember wherever you are and whatever you're doing.

When you think, 'I can't do this'/ 'I'm a failure' / 'I'm not good enough', it's very easy to just accept these thoughts as facts and feel crap about them. They are thoughts, not facts. They are your negatively skewed brain's opinions and evaluations. They do not represent reality.

We want you to become more aware of these types of thought so you can challenge and then change them. For example, 'I'm a failure' should become 'I think I'm a failure.' It's a fundamental difference which will encourage you not to just accept this kind of thinking as factual without any proof. Okay, you think you've failed or are going to fail: ask yourself these questions:

+ What abilities and skills do you have that might enable you to succeed?
+ Upon what scale are you judging success and failure?
+ Have you ever managed to do something similar in the past?
+ What proof do you have both for and against this thought?

Whenever you next catch yourself indulging thoughts masquerading as facts, try to discredit them. You'll no doubt be surprised by how often you put yourself down with all-encompassing statements that are in fact total nonsense, encouraging you to think, 'Well, actually I think I did that quite well,' or 'X, Y and Z seemed to like it so maybe it wasn't so bad.'

Next steps ...

CBT will help you to:

✦ Develop a more realistic perception of yourself based upon a fairer interpretation of events

✦ Update your thinking so you are less self-critical and can question the validity of negative thoughts

✦ Stop punishing yourself for perceived failures

✦ Give you faith in your abilities, your strengths and your skills

✦ Encourage you to try things you've been putting off or have dismissed as 'too hard'

✦ Increase your feelings of self-worth and self-belief

✦ Set and achieve both short-term and long-term goals

Thoughts to take away

✓ How confident you feel depends on your interpretation of an event. Viewing things more realistically will boost your self-esteem

✓ The way you think, behave and feel physically and emotionally are all interlinked – if you change one for the better the rest will follow

✓ Be fair on yourself. Be aware of your tendency to only focus on the negatives. Start looking for the positives too

3

I Think,
Therefore
I Am

Everyone has a little voice in their head that lets them know how they're getting on. If yours is constantly telling you you're rubbish then it's time to shut it up and get a more helpful and realistic view.

Your inner judge and jury

Everyone has a tiny judge residing in their head who pipes up every now and then with pearls of so-called 'wisdom'. Rather than encouraging you when you're feeling insecure and shouting, 'You're doing really well,' your inner judge is far more likely to berate and belittle you. You'll typically hear things like, 'You're never going to manage,' or 'You're not good enough,' rather than anything remotely helpful or motivating. This kind of thinking will have a huge effect on how you feel emotionally and physically and how you behave.

When the running commentary in your mind is negatively skewed (which it always will be when you're suffering from LSE) you'll beat yourself up for every (perceived) mistake, condemning yourself for not measuring up to the all-singing, all-dancing vision of perfection that your very own judge thinks you should be.

This judge is incredibly convincing because they will only ever focus on, and seem to confirm, long-held beliefs you hold about yourself. For example, if you've always felt overweight and physically unattractive your judge will dwell exhaustively on those topics, picking out instances when you felt your worst and expounding on them until all sense of perspective is lost. Each of these thoughts chips away at your self-esteem until you don't feel strong enough or 'good enough' to try to prove them wrong.

There is a big difference between focusing solely on your faults and assessing them realistically. If you complete 99 per cent of a task well, but mess up 1 per cent you'll spend all your time musing on the smaller proportion – which is ridiculous. It's important to step back from a situation and take a view of the whole picture, not just what went wrong. A fair view would be to give 99 per cent of your attention to what went right and 1 per cent to what went wrong. People tend to learn more when they are praised and encouraged, so while you shouldn't totally ignore your faults you need to keep them in proportion.

Our inner judges spew out thoughts known as negative automatic thoughts – or NATs. They're hideously vindictive and they'll whizz through your head without you even noticing.

Negative automatic thoughts

NATs are the thoughts we mentioned in Chapter 2 that disguise themselves as facts. Things like, 'I'm not clever enough,' and 'I can't cope with this.' They're 'automatic' because they flash through your mind – uninvited – too fleeting for proper consideration. They appear and disappear as quickly as a Tasmanian Devil, leaving untold damage in their wake. NATs are responsible for maintaining your negative default view of yourself, creating the biases that distort information to fit your fears and self-doubt.

The trouble with NATs is that they're often plausible (for example, you might be struggling to cope with something), but they'll always be unreasonable and unrealistic (there are ways and means to cope). If you catch a NAT before it disappears and analyse it, you'll realise it's completely ludicrous. However, it's more likely that it will appear reasonable to you at the time because of your low opinion of yourself: 'Of course I can't cope, I'm weak and stupid.' This will make you feel terrible emotionally and physically – and will cause you to act in unhelpful ways (e.g. by avoiding tackling a problem or by hiding away).

Typical (but often totally unconscious) responses to NATs include:

+ Having an extreme view of success or failure based on perfectionism. There'll be no middle ground – okay isn't good enough.

+ A tendency to move the goalposts so you can never meet your own crazy expectations.

+ Ignoring any successes or playing them down, instead dwelling on what you did wrong. 'Yes, I won that award, but it was a fluke. The woman/guy that should have won left the company.'

+ Being suggestible: you mould criticism you hear about others to reflect yourself, so if a friend tells you her mother-in-law constantly undermines her parenting skills, you'll start questioning your own parenting skills.

+ Your thoughts will be peppered with negatively biased words like 'should' or 'shouldn't', e.g. 'I should have asked him out for a drink,' or 'I shouldn't have asked him out for a drink.' This suggests a failing in your decision-making skills. More positively-minded people will favour the far more neutral 'can' or 'will', e.g. 'I can ask him next time,' or 'I won't ask him next time.'

+ You'll make sweeping generalisations about yourself based on specific events. For example, if you don't get a job it's because 'I never get offered jobs', 'I'm useless', 'I never learn', and consequently, 'everything is ruined'.

+ You'll shape compliments to fit your negative view. For instance if someone says you've done a great job, you'll wonder if you don't come up to scratch the rest of the time.

'Average' is not in your vocab. You're either doing badly or terribly.

You're never doing okay or – heaven forbid – well. (Newsflash: 'perfect' doesn't exist. No, not even that ridiculously athletic man next door with the great wife, kids and job is perfect. He's probably knee-deep in debt and having an affair.) You don't support yourself through compassion, encouragement or praise. It's a vicious circle because feeling this way makes you act in uncertain, tentative or unhelpful ways which actually prompts the bad outcome you feared, leading to thoughts like, 'There I go again' or 'Typical! That's just like me.'

The NAT mind map

The NAT mind map below shows the influence NATs have on how you feel physically, emotionally and what they'll make you do or want to do.

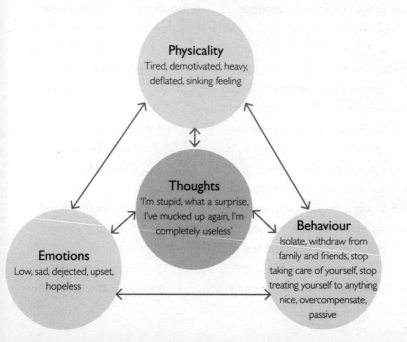

⑤ Tracking NATs

Becoming aware of NATs so you can really see and understand the damage they're doing will help you start formulating more healthy interpretations of situations.

For one day we want you to catch as many NATs as you can and write them down. Every time you find yourself questioning or berating yourself, note down the thoughts going through your head. Then write down how this thought made you feel emotionally and physically and what it made you do or think about doing. Because there might be a lot of them it will be easier to fill in a table rather than individual mind maps. We've included a few examples in the table below.

NAT	Emotion	Physicality	Behaviour
'I'm never going to get the job'	Resigned	Sluggish, tired	Avoid prepping for the interview
'Claire is so much more stylish than me'	Embarrassed, frustrated	Tense, hunched	Wear deliberately nondescript clothes
'I can't leave him because no one else will have me'	Distressed, angry, frightened	Suffer from constant headaches and stomach cramps	Over- or under-eating, avoiding social occasions

When you've completed the table for one day, look over all your NATs. Is there a common thread running through them all (i.e. are they all concerned with work, your relationship, your job or your appearance)?

Or are they very broad, covering lots of topics? This might be the first time you've actually consciously engaged with these thoughts so seeing them written down could be quite shocking. Perhaps you didn't realise that a lot of your insecurity is focused on your work or your relationship or quite how often you're being mean to yourself. Realising this will give your NAT battles some focus – you've identified what particular areas you're more likely to dwell on negatively, so you will be more wary of those thoughts in the future, rather than just accepting them and moving on to the next.

Self-criticism pros and cons

You may have convinced yourself that you achieve more when you're pushed, cajoled and bullied, but you're actually far more likely to feel motivated if you credit yourself for your achievements and effort. If you were on a sports team what kind of coach would you rather have – one who only screamed abuse and never took your progress into account or one who said encouraging things like, 'That wasn't great … but you can do better,' and 'Well done, you've really improved'? You can even picture what they might look like: furious, red-faced and ready to punch a wall versus cheerful, calm and enthusiastic. We'd much rather hang out with the second option.

⑤ Your inner judge's pros and cons

Make a list of all the pros and cons of having a self-righteous pain in the arse bully as an inner judge. Feel free to add to the example over the page:

Pros	Cons
✦ None. Zero. Zilch. Bupkis. Nada. No deal.	✦ It makes me feel low and not good enough ✦ It makes me frightened to try new things ✦ It makes me expect to fail

Now make a list of the pros and cons of having a fair and reasonable inner judge:

Pros	Cons
✦ I feel motivated and driven ✦ I'm encouraged to try new things ✦ I won't apologise for myself all the time ✦ I feel like I can cope in stressful situations	✦ I can't beat myself up any more ✦ I can't hide away from challenges ✦ I can't self-sabotage

The last three cons (and this whole exercise) should show you how your own beliefs and actions maintain negative thinking, but when you start thinking more fairly your fear of failure will vanish. Those last three cons will cease to exist.

Challenging NATs

Now you're more aware of NATs and what they're up to, you're in a much better position to challenge them. For the next week, fill in the form opposite whenever you notice yourself feeling insecure, sad, anxious, hopeless or guilty. Emotional changes are an obvious indication that something more's going on – in this instance a NAT. Write down the trigger (what caused this thought?), then assess how strongly you believe the NAT (0–100, where 0 is not at all and 100 is completely). How did it make you feel and then how did you behave?

Next up is the really important bit. Write down how you can

challenge the thought. Is it an opinion or a fact? How else can you view the situation? If you're struggling to to disprove the NAT then ask yourself what you'd tell a friend who was in your position.

After you've really considered this new way of thinking assess how much you believe the original NAT now (0–100) and what a balanced and more realistic perspective on the situation would be.

⑤ Your NAT challenge

We have filled out some examples to help you get started.

Situation	Not understanding what people are talking about	Feeling unattractive at a social event
Self-critical thought	'You're an idiot. You can't ask them to clarify as you'll look stupid'	'You've put on weight and look run-down and everyone has noticed'
How strongly do I believe this? (0–100)	80	100
Emotion	Sad, embarrassed, ashamed	Angry, frustrated
Behaviour	Stay quiet, don't say anything to avoid showing myself up	Wear big baggy clothes, cover face with my hands, constantly check what I look like in my compact mirror
Challenges to self-criticism	I joined the conversation half way through. Just because I don't know what they're talking about it doesn't mean I'm stupid!	Yes, I have put on weight, but lots of people look great my size. Buying clothes that fit and flatter my shape will make me feel more confident
How much do you believe the original thought now? (0–100)	50	70
What would a more balanced perspective be?	It would be unusual if I did immediately grasp a conversation I've only just joined. I could wait until I can guess from what they're saying	I can still look great whatever size I am and no one will be paying as much attention to me as I am

Filling in the table will have got easier throughout the week as you became better at spotting NATs and confronting them. Practice makes perfect. The more you stop these thoughts and demand proof the less automatic they'll become and the less influence they'll have over you. You're doing all the right things to stop your inner judge spouting unfounded rubbish. You're not letting ridiculous opinions of yourself interfere with how you live your life.

Keep using the table for the next week (and the week after and the week after that). The more determined you are to question your inner critic, the quieter it'll become. Giving yourself distance from the situations and your thoughts will offer up alternative perspectives – more positive and realistic ones.

Being compassionate to yourself

Your compassionate side is pretty much dead in the water as far as you're concerned. You would never dream of speaking to anyone else like you speak to yourself. If someone else was feeling low you wouldn't be judgemental, you'd try to help them find a way around whatever problem they were facing. So why is there one rule for them and one for you? As twee as it sounds, you need to find a new compassionate voice for yourself.

⑤ Capturing compassion

This strategy is about shutting up your inner judge and learning how to talk to yourself in a far more warm and helpful way, as if you really care about and believe in yourself (because you do really, underneath all that fear and doubt). Follow these steps, jotting down your answers:

Think of someone who is warm, fair, wise and strong. Someone who isn't judgemental and whose opinion you trust. You might know them personally (i.e. a family member, a friend or a colleague) or just someone that you admire.

✦ Make a list of the positive qualities they possess. Are they driven? A good mediator? Kind? Fun? A good listener?

✦ How do they talk? (Bear with us, this has a point.) Do they speak slowly or quickly? Is their tone low or high-pitched? Are they generally loud or quiet?

✦ What kind of things can you imagine them saying to you if you told them some of your NATs? How would they reassure you, show you your good qualities and generally be encouraging?

What you've written down will form the basis for your new inner voice. When you're next in a difficult situation where self-criticism usually kicks in stop, take a moment and consciously choose to talk to yourself in the way you've described above (even down to imagining the tone and pitch). So, rather than hearing a miserable and bitter old grump you'll be hearing a compassionate and inspiring motivator. This will make you feel more in control of your thoughts which, coupled with the positive stuff you'll be hearing in your head, will make you feel more confident.

Reflect rather than ruminate

So, something went wrong or things didn't pan out exactly as you'd hoped. What happens now? Well, you have two options. You can either:

1 **Ruminate:** Dwell on what went wrong, what mistakes you made and what you could have done differently aggravating NATs such as, 'I failed' or 'I was useless', so you end up feeling terrible.

2 **Reflect:** Work out what went wrong and what went right. Identify why some things worked and some things didn't and make a plan for next time.

Obviously option 2 is the much healthier route as ruminating on anything is a total and utter waste of time. You can't change the past, but you can learn from it.

⑤ Reflecting and planning

+ **Think back to a recent experience where you feel you fell short or made a mistake.** I behaved badly at a big office party, drinking too much and ignoring some people.

+ **Make a list of five things (yes – five) that went well or that you managed okay.** I made my boss laugh, I complimented the girl who'd organised it, I had a good conversation with one of the directors, I made a good contact from another department and I helped tidy up.

+ **Now, list what went wrong (There's no minimum or maximum number).** My colleague was moaning about her job (which is much better than mine) and I laughed at her. I then just walked away and didn't explain myself. I thought she was being really insensitive.

+ **What could you change or work on for next time?** I could call her, apologise and explain how I'm having a terrible time at work so took what she said badly. Also, I could really listen to why she's hating her job (perhaps it's not as great as I think it is?) and maybe offer some advice. If we're both going through the same perhaps we could help each other?

+ **Do you need to ask for help?** I could ask an objective friend or colleague what they think and what the best approach should be.

+ **Ask yourself, 'Will what I'm worrying about matter in a day, a month or a year from now?'** No. My colleague isn't a mind reader so doesn't know what I was thinking; she probably didn't even notice my behaviour. However, if she did she won't dwell on it for longer than a day or so.

Facing things that you're worried about head-on will make you feel more in control, which will automatically make you feel more confident about your ability to deal with them.

Thoughts to take away

✓ Identifying and then challenging NATs will prove that there are alternative ways of viewing situations

✓ Ask yourself, 'What would I tell a friend if they were in the same situation?' You're always going to be fairer to a friend than yourself

✓ You can choose to change your inner voice so it's more realistic, impartial and compassionate

4

Fortune Favours the Brave

Making wild conjectures about the potentially hideous consequences of your actions is pretty standard when you feel insecure, but that doesn't make it okay. This chapter will convince you that anxious predictions are a waste of time and head space.

The angst of anxious predictions

When you're feeling unconfident you're more likely to predict the worst – to look into the future and only see doom and gloom. Thoughts like, 'I can't do that, it's too hard' and 'I'm not experienced enough, I'll make a fool of myself,' will make starting anything new or tackling obstacles seem impossible and overwhelming.

Making predictions about the future and assessing what might or might not happen is a survival technique. Back in the days of dinosaurs and animal-skin skirts, cave people had to analyse the danger of certain situations and work out whether wrestling that mammoth would be foolhardy. Our danger sensors are as sensitive today as they ever were. If we didn't assess risk there would be nothing to stop us leaping off bridges for laughs or telling our boss exactly what we think of them. Acknowledging the parameters for success and failure are what stops society imploding. Which is all well and good … until your predictions and assessments don't reflect reality, which is what happens when you're suffering from LSE.

When you lack confidence and self-belief you'll generate a million potential negative scenarios that might result from something you do or say (or not do or say), while ignoring any positive ones. These negative predictions will make you feel anxious, nervous and uncertain. Anxiety tricks you into believing things are more threatening than they really are. Your confidence nosedives and you can physically tense up as your body goes into fight or flight mode.

Fight or flight

When you feel threatened your instinctual fight or flight response is triggered sending adrenaline and cortisol flooding into your blood stream. Your heart beats faster, pumping blood away from the areas that don't need it to the muscles and limbs that will either be fighting or running away. Your breathing will increase, forcing more oxygen into your bloodstream, your pupils will dilate to sharpen your sight, your hearing will become pin-drop sharp and your perception of pain diminishes. The part of your brain that looks after rational, everyday stuff will take a back seat so you can focus fully on the danger.

You are in 'attack mode' – ideal if you're dodging bullets in a James Bond-style car chase, but not so great if you're just feeling a little insecure about asking for a pay rise.

Your body cannot differentiate between physical threats (i.e. a car chase or an earthquake) and psychological ones (i.e. asking for a pay rise or having to face your ex at a party). It'll react just the same and your mind will start actively hunting out any other potential threats, deliberately focusing on any and all negatives.

Common anxious predictions

When your confidence is at rock bottom and you feel anxious, your predictions about the future will include either one of or all of the below:

✦ An overestimation on the likelihood of failure. You'll think things won't work out how you want them to or how others want them to and you'll assume that the worst is inevitable.

✦ An exaggeration about the repercussions of something going wrong, i.e. it'll be disastrous and reflect terribly on you.

✦ An underestimation of your ability to cope with things if they don't go according to plan.

✦ A complete disregard for anything that suggests it won't be a failure. Even if you once succeeded before at the exact same thing, you'll ignore this or deliberately make that situation different somehow so it can't be used comparatively.

Your anxiety might directly contribute to the problem if it makes you too fearful to ask for help or feedback, leaving you with no measure of how you're doing or how you might perform. Instead, you have to base all of your assumptions on what's going on in your head.

If you let predictions like Julia's go unchallenged they will have a big impact on your life, affecting how you feel and what you do. Even when you do succeed and do well you'll undermine your performance and focus on any possible downsides, e.g. 'Yes, but it can't last,' or 'It was a fluke – I managed by the skin of my teeth.' By only focusing on the negatives of her current situation Julia was ignoring how brilliant it was that she'd managed two whole years juggling three jobs. If she

Example: Julia's faulty professional foresight

The company where Julia worked had been hit hard by the recession. 15 per cent of staff had been laid off in the last two years and everyone who'd survived the cull felt lucky to still have a job. Well, kind of. Julia knew she should feel grateful, but her workload had trebled, she was in the office fourteen hours a day and she could see no light at the end of the tunnel. There was a recruitment freeze so she knew she wouldn't be getting help anytime soon, but after two solid years of this with no let-up she was completely and utterly exhausted.

She was starting to fall behind and had already been reprimanded twice by her boss. She couldn't understand how she was expected to continue at this pace with no support or at least a pay rise to both compensate her for the increased responsibility and reward her for it. She felt unappreciated … but then also ashamed. Shouldn't she be thankful just to be working?

She'd been meaning to speak to her boss about it for six months now, but she knew it was a bad idea. Her boss would be angry, disappointed and would think even less of her than she did now. They wouldn't be able to get her an assistant and she wouldn't get a pay rise so what was the point?

Julia's mind map looks like this:

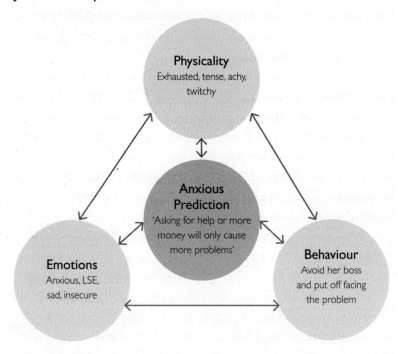

Physicality
Exhausted, tense, achy, twitchy

Anxious Prediction
'Asking for help or more money will only cause more problems'

Emotions
Anxious, LSE, sad, insecure

Behaviour
Avoid her boss and put off facing the problem

started congratulating rather than berating herself it would make her feel more confident about approaching her boss. When you're thinking fearfully your predictions don't get updated because you discount anything that doesn't fit with your pessimistic view. Inevitably your behaviour will reflect this and, like Julia, you'll end up either putting off facing your problems, or avoiding them altogether.

Avoidance and procrastination

Fear can make you avoid or put off making changes and the longer you run away from issues the harder and more frightening they become until they seem insurmountable.

If you don't face something you'll never get the chance to disprove your negative predictions. You'll never be able to discover whether you can cope or whether things might change for the better. Take Julia: if she'd asked her boss for help what's the worst that might happen? Her boss says 'no'. However, she might also say, 'I appreciate everything you're doing and things will change in two months as the recruitment freeze is lifting.' Julia would then feel appreciated and relieved, knowing that things are going to change.

Avoidance or procrastination might seem easier at the time, but in reality they're just adding to your insecurity and throwing guilt into the mix too. There is never a 'perfect' time to do things. There'll always be an excuse or a reason not to if you look for one, but the more you put it off the harder it will be to confront. You'll then feel guilty for not having addressed things sooner and will have to deal with thoughts like, 'I've made my bed now so I have to lie in it,' or 'It's too late to make changes.'

Procrastination also prompts self-sabotage. Often you'll leave something until the last minute because you're frightened of failing or of not being good enough. If things do go wrong you can then say, 'Well, I would have done better had I worked harder or done it sooner.'

You also might start something, but quit if it gets too difficult or if you think you're not doing well enough. Or you'll over-prepare. You'll be so worried about not doing well enough that you try to cover all

Example: Craig's weight concerns

Craig had wanted to lose weight for years, but he'd always been too embarrassed to ask for help so would look up faddy diets online, try them for a couple of weeks and then give up. His track record in starting and failing had put him off trying again, but his weight was creeping up and up. He felt embarrassed and insecure about his appearance.

He'd grown out of all his clothes and had stopped sitting down next to people on buses and trains because he didn't want to encroach on their space. He felt horrible, but didn't know what to do. 'I'll just mess up another diet as I have no will power and then I'll feel worse,' he told himself. When he felt this low he would start comfort eating and it turned into a vicious circle.

possible bases and, rather than feeling ready for anything, you end up exhausted and worried that you may have missed something. And, if it does go well, you'll put it down to all the preparation you did rather than your skill and natural ability.

Only by facing the things you fear will you realise that you can do them and you can cope. Take the example above, Craig keeps ruminating on his past defeats. Instead he should reflect on what happened before so he can work out what went wrong and use that knowledge to help him do things differently this time.

Craig's mind map looks like this:

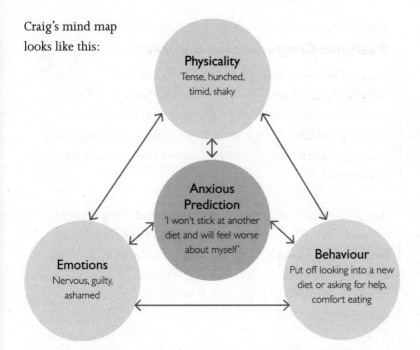

Physicality
Tense, hunched, timid, shaky

Anxious Prediction
'I won't stick at another diet and will feel worse about myself'

Behaviour
Put off looking into a new diet or asking for help, comfort eating

Emotions
Nervous, guilty, ashamed

Challenging anxious predictions

Even confident people feel nervous about how things will go. The difference is that they have enough faith in themselves to believe both that things will work out okay and that even if they don't they'll be able to cope with the fallout. Feeling anxious won't determine a negative or positive outcome – what you do determines what actually happens. Remember: your thoughts aren't magic. Just like you can't think your way into winning the lottery, you can't think your way into looking foolish or looking great. It's what you do that matters.

Just as you challenged your NATs, you need to challenge your anxious predictions to convince your panicky brain that these are just hypotheses, not facts. You're not a fortune teller, you can't predict the future. Basing your decisions on anxious predictions is a corrosive habit – one that you need to break.

Ⓢ The anxious prediction table

Fill in the table below with any anxious predictions you have during the next week. Next to your prediction mark down how much you believe it will happen (0–100). Evaluate the assumption and put it in perspective: what evidence do you have for and against it? Is there a more credible and realistic view?

Filling in the table will prove to you that your worst-case scenario thoughts are ridiculously unrealistic, but even if the worst does happen

Situation	Giving a presentation at work	Asking my friend to look after the kids for a few hours last minute
What is/are my anxious prediction(s) and how much do I believe they will happen (0–100)?	I'll go red (80) I'll stutter (70) I won't be able to do it (70) People will laugh (65) I'll lose my job (30)	She'll think I'm disorganised (95) She'll say no and I'll have looked bad for nothing (85) She'll judge my parenting skills (75)
How do your predictions make you feel emotionally?	Anxious Nervous Panicky	Embarrassed Indebted Guilty
What is the evidence for my predictions ...	I have never done a presentation at work before At school I was terrible at public speaking I stutter when I'm nervous	There is no evidence to support my prediction, it's just I've never asked my friend for help before

What is the evidence against my predictions?	The presentation is just in front of my team and they all like me so they'll want it to be a success. They're not going to try to trip me up or put me off. I probably will feel a bit nervous, but that's normal and it's just because I care and want things to go well	My friend is lovely and we get on really well. She's offered to look after the children for me in the past, I've just never taken her up on it. Even if she is unsure about taking the kids, I can explain why and let her know that it's an emergency and that I wouldn't normally ask
What is the worst that could happen?	I muck up and don't manage to finish the presentation, people laugh at me and I'll be reprimanded	She doesn't take the children and says she's shocked that I've got myself into this situation
If the worst happens what could I do to cope?	If people do laugh I can try to see the funny side too and put on a brave face. They would only do it in a good-natured way. If I was reprimanded I could ask for some training in public speaking so I can get better	If she says 'no' I could ask someone else, see if I can take the kids with me or try to rearrange the last-minute plan. If she looks surprised at the suddenness I'll explain again that this is a one-off
What is the best that could happen?	It could go brilliantly and everyone will be really impressed with me	She's happy to take the children and they have a good time together
What is the most likely thing that will happen?	I do the presentation and feel nervous, but it goes okay	She will take the children to help me out
How likely would you rate your predictions now (0–100)?	I'll go red (80) I'll stutter (50) I won't be able to do it (20) People will laugh (20) I'll lose my job (0)	She'll think I'm disorganised (40) She'll say no and I'll have looked bad for nothing (10) She'll judge my parenting skills (0)

you'll be able to cope. Dissecting your predictions will break down the feeling of fear (which can seem overwhelming) into its component parts giving you the opportunity to deal with each worry individually, reducing your insecurity and building your confidence. You'll be able to approach situations with an open mind. If you keep using this table whenever you find anxious predictions getting you down challenging these kind of thoughts will quickly become second nature. Soon you won't even have to use the table, realistically assessing a situation will be something you can do quickly in your head and you'll naturally approach tasks with more confidence.

Imagining success

When you're panicking about possible hideous outcomes it's natural to imagine the scenario playing out in your head. Imagery is a powerful thing. If you can imagine yourself stuttering and stumbling during that presentation and you hear people laughing at you it can seem inevitable that it'll happen. Imagining these scenes makes you feel all the same emotions and physical responses that you would if it were actually happening. You feel ashamed, embarrassed and petrified before you've even started.

At the moment you're very well practised at visualising catastrophic things happening, but terrible at picturing good things. We want you to use imagery to run through all the possible positive outcomes of an event so you're seeing, hearing and feeling success instead of failure. Also, you'll naturally have to run through all the things you need to do to ensure it goes well – it's like a rehearsal. Athletes and actors often practise this technique before competing or performing. It puts their mind and body in the best possible place to recreate in reality exactly what they just saw in their head.

Imagery will help you to:

+ Familiarise yourself with what you need to do so you feel well-prepared

✦ Build your confidence before trying something new
✦ Reduce negative thoughts by concentrating on positive outcomes
✦ Aim for success because you've already seen and tasted it!

⑤ Your successful imagery exercise

Think of something you need to do or face in the next week, couple of weeks or the next month. Something that's been worrying you, bothering you and that you've been making anxious predictions about.

1 Write down the specific issue or situation that is bothering you.
✦ I need to break up with my emotionally abusive boyfriend without allowing him to bully me into staying.

2 Next, jot down the best-case scenario for how everything plays out. What you would do, what would others do and what's your preferred final result?
✦ I would tell him firmly that this is my decision and that it is final. I would also stress how this is the best thing for both of us – neither of us are happy and we're just becoming unhappier as the days go on. He would be upset, but would accept my decision and let me leave.

3 Read it out loud. Hearing the words will make your determination to see this through more official. It will also give you some distance from your thoughts so you might spot another step in the plan or a resolution to an obstacle that you'd previously missed.
✦ If he shouts, I will repeat firmly and calmly that this is my final decision and that it is for the best. I will refuse to be drawn into an

argument or into any kind of blame game. I will just say, 'This is what has to happen for the good of us both.'

4 Close your eyes, clear your mind and take some deep breaths, breathing in through your nose and out through your mouth.

5 Now picture the most confident version of yourself you can imagine. It's you on your best ever day. What are you wearing, how are you standing and are you ready?

✦ I will stand confidently with my head held high and I'll also have my bag packed and ready to go so I don't have to quickly pack while he's upset. Having things ready will convince him I'm absolutely certain of my decision and I'm not going to change my mind.

6 Physically echo the posture and stance of this version of you. Lower your shoulders, stand tall and keep your chin up.

7 Run through exactly what you want to happen – every last detail – in your head. What does this confident version of you say, do, think and feel? It's a movie and you're the director. You are in total control.

8 Watch yourself succeed exactly as you want to.

To make the most out of imagery you need to practise it, so go over and over this scene as many times as you need to until the positivity has transferred into real life.

Visualisation like this will help convince you that things can go well and that you can make changes. As frightening as it is to confront problems you do have the skills and inner strength to see them through. You don't have to settle for feeling constantly worried, anxious and unfulfilled.

The next chapter will show you how to put your new-found confidence and self-belief into practice.

Thoughts to take away

✓ Swapping anxious predictions for realistic and balanced ones will boost your confidence more than you can imagine

✓ Use visualisation techniques to get into a positive and confident frame of mind

✓ Carry the image of you at your best in your head and ask yourself, 'What would this version of me do?' whenever you feel anxious or unsure

5

Actions Speak Louder Than Thoughts

Now your thoughts aren't working so hard against you, it's time to face your fears and take action. By actually doing the things you've been putting off, you'll soon realise that they're not nearly as terrifying as you'd built them up to be.

Acting out

Now you're an expert on challenging both NATs and anxious predictions, you can test out the shiny new confident version of you that's alive and well in your imagination. You need to start facing the things you've been shying away from so you can prove to yourself that you can cope and you are good enough.

When you suffer from LSE your NATs and anxious predictions may well have tried to convince you that if something goes wrong it's because there's something fundamentally wrong with you, rather than it being the result of a lack of confidence, practice or unfortunate circumstances. Now you're starting to have a more realistic view of what can happen – and what's most likely to happen – you'll feel more confident in your ability to not only start tasks, but to complete them. Finishing something you've been putting off will give you a massive boost of confidence and motivation, regardless of whether it went okay, well or brilliantly – the point is you did it!

Sussing out self-efficacy

Psychologist Albert Bandura defined self-efficacy as 'a belief in your ability to succeed in certain situations'. This belief (or lack thereof) plays a major role in how you approach tasks, challenges and goals.

People with low self-efficacy tend to wait until they feel completely certain about something before doing it – which normally means they wait a very long time (forever, in some cases). To build self-esteem you need to get used to taking action before you're completely ready – like confident people do. They know they can deal with the fallout if things go wrong, but they have enough faith in themselves to believe they

The self-efficacy rules

People with a strong sense of self-efficacy:

+ View challenges as tasks to be mastered
+ Develop a deep interest in activities in which they're involved
+ Form a sense of commitment and attachment to what they're doing
+ Recover quickly from setbacks and disappointments

People with a weak sense of self-efficacy:

+ Avoid challenging tasks
+ Believe that difficult situations and activities are beyond their capabilities
+ Focus on personal failings and negative outcomes
+ Quickly lose confidence in their personal skills

won't have to.

So far you've just been thinking about making changes, which is brilliant and a great first step. But you need to put everything you've learned into practice. It's only once you've started something that you have any hope of finishing it. Your stress levels will reduce dramatically once you've actually begun.

You have to put yourself in situations that you might find scary to stop yourself getting stuck in a rut. This will enable you to get feedback and to prove that you can cope, which will raise both your confidence, self-esteem and self-efficacy levels.

Tried and tested

The last chapter concentrated on challenging your thoughts and predictions surrounding events or situations so you have a more realistic view of your abilities and of what might happen. Now you can find out what actually will happen. You need to test out your new positive ways of thinking to collate evidence that your inner judge won't be able to dismiss.

⑤ Putting self-efficacy to the test

We have modified the table you used in the previous chapter to challenge your anxious predictions. This time you're actually going to do what scares you or what you've been avoiding so you can prove several things to yourself:

1 That you can face difficult tasks
2 That negative predictions hardly ever come true, but if they do …
3 You can cope if things go wrong
4 That thinking more realistically about what will happen will make you feel more confident

Putting everything you've learned so far into practice (see over the page), follow the simple guidelines below:

✦ Make a list of all the things you've been putting off or that you're feeling anxious about.
✦ Rank each of the tasks, events or situations in order of difficulty or fear levels starting with the easiest/least scary first and building up to the most difficult/most frightening.
✦ Being as detailed as possible write down the least intimidating task/

event in the situation box.

+ Next, note down what you predict will happen. How will you feel when you do it, what do you think other people might notice, etc.? Then, just like you did in the last chapter, rate the prediction according to how much you believe it'll actually happen on a scale of 0–100. (Hopefully these predictions won't be as apocalyptic as they once might have been after all your work so far.)

+ Devise an experiment to test your prediction. What can you do to best find out if your prediction will come true?

+ Conduct the experiment, face your fear and complete the task.

+ Write down what actually happened. How did this compare to what you were expecting? What did you learn? What impact did acting differently have on how you felt? What implications does this have on your negative view of yourself? You may find that your anxious predictions were not correct and that the alternatives you found were more realistic and helpful. Or you may discover that your anxious predictions were spot-on, but that you dealt with them just fine

+ Gradually work through your list. Remember to ignore any 'I don't want to do this' or 'I can't be bothered' feelings. They're trying to trick you into not giving this your best shot. Actually facing your fears is the only way to prove you are capable and to feel better. The more you do, the easier it will become to face each task.

Before you start, identify any unhelpful behaviours that you might engage in to cope with your negative predictions and anxiety (e.g. avoidance, escape, over-preparing) and make sure you ban yourself from doing these during the experiment.

We have filled out a couple of examples to start you off.

Situation	Prediction	Experiment	Outcome	Conclusion
	What do you think will happen and to what extent do you believe it will (0–100)?	How can you test out these predictions?	What actually happened?	Was your prediction correct? Is there a more balanced view? How do you feel about your predictions now?
Going on a second date with a man/ woman I really like	They'll find me boring if I haven't had anything to drink (95) They won't want to go out again (100)	The last date was really boozy, so I deliberately won't drink too much to see how it goes. I won't ask them out but will wait to see if they contact me	I didn't drink too much and had a brilliant time. He/ she hasn't asked me out again yet, but I think they will	They didn't find me boring, we had a right laugh. My predictions seem a bit silly. Even if he/ she doesn't ask me out again, I'll know it's not because of anything I did or didn't do on the date
Asking for a promotion and pay rise	They'll say no and list all my faults (75) They'll accuse me of being greedy (80) They'll think I'm overreaching myself (80)	Schedule the meeting and ask. Make sure I'm prepared with a list of reasons as to why I deserve it	They said no, but stressed that they appreciate everything I'm doing and know how hard I work. They said they'll review the situation in three months	Even if they did think I was overreaching myself, I think they respected me for asking and see me as ambitious in a good way now. I also feel better knowing they appreciate my work

Actually putting your fears and insecurities to the test should have proved to you that things rarely ever go as badly as you think they will and, even if they do, you have the skills to cope with the consequences. Reward yourself and give yourself some credit for actually completing this strategy. Taking action and facing up to your fears is incredibly brave and you should be proud of yourself. Not only have you faced your fears, but you've disproved your worst self-criticisms. Your inner judge will now have either changed his tune dramatically or packed up and left.

The principle of perfection

Perfection doesn't exist. It's a dangerous myth. We've already mentioned this, but it bears repeating because trying to measure up to some idealistic vision of what you think you should be or what you think others think you should be is a one-way ticket to LSE Central.

Confidence is all about knowing you can cope with whatever life throws at you – good or bad. And by 'cope' we mean succeed in the best way possible for you at the time. You have to be realistic about what you can and can't do and what is likely to happen. Which can be hard if you feel you're lacking in some way. While pushing yourself to achieve more can be a good thing, don't use it as a whip to punish yourself.

Making mistakes and failing isn't a weakness. It's part and parcel of learning, growing and understanding yourself better. The pressure you'll put yourself under by demanding perfection will make you a nervous wreck. The stakes will be so high that every experience will become something to be endured rather than enjoyed. Also, if you're on a quest for perfection your own internal rules will dictate that you can never win. You'll constantly move the goalposts: your new partner doesn't quite tick all the boxes; your £1,000 pay rise should have been £3,000; your 5lb weight loss should have been 7lb. Give yourself a break!

You may also stop working hard, start procrastinating or avoiding things out of the misguided belief that if you try and don't achieve everything you wanted you'll have failed in some way. Don't let fear get in the way of grasping new opportunities. Perfection is a delusion and disappointment is only temporary. Mistakes are part and parcel of taking risks, they help you test the limit of your ideas and can inspire creativity and innovation. They are a necessary part of self-development, enabling you to hone new skills and understand yourself and others better.

Leaving your comfort zone

Depending on how long you've suffered from LSE and low confidence you might have got quite comfortable putting things off, avoiding them or not trying as hard as you could. Settling for a life half lived is an option, but it's not the best one or the right one. You might think hiding away and not reaching your full potential or challenging yourself makes things easier. It doesn't: in the long run you have to live with your feelings of guilt, regret and insecurity. When things don't work out as you'd expected or as you'd wanted them to, it can be very difficult, but using that as the basis for how you then live your life is a cop-out. You can make changes. You are strong enough so why choose not to? What are you gaining by avoiding any risks? A safe life maybe, but is it a happy and fulfilled one? There is nothing stopping you from trying.

Update your personal rules

Imagine how liberating it would be to stop caring about failing. The ridiculous thing is that by taking the pressure off yourself you're actually far more likely to do your best. You need to change your personal rules from 'anything less than perfect = failure' to 'I'll try my best and learn from whatever the outcome is.'

Example: A course for concern

Robyn had worked as a teaching assistant in a junior school for six months and loved it. All the staff said she'd be a great teacher and encouraged her to apply for the full-time course starting in six months. Feeling excited and motivated she took their advice and applied. She filled out all the forms, went to all the interviews and nervously waited to see if she'd made the course.

She didn't.

She was mortified. Not only did she feel as though she'd let herself down, but she also felt like she'd let all her colleagues down too. They'd all helped her and pushed her and she felt they would be as disappointed as she was. She cried when she told them she hadn't made it – and then she felt bad for making them feel sad. ⋯⋰

⋯⋮ Not getting on the course shattered her confidence. She withdrew and became quieter at work and made silly mistakes that she never would have made before. 'If I'm not good enough for the course, I'm clearly not good enough to be an assistant,' she thought. Physically she was tense, riled up, fidgety and nervous and she started avoiding the staff room at breaks and lunchtimes.

Practice makes perfect

It's a cliché, but it's also true. If you've made a mistake or something didn't go as well as you wanted, just practise. Learn from what went wrong last time and practise until you're confident enough to try again.

If you're scared of public speaking give dozens of speeches until you feel at ease. Speak to the mirror, to your partner, to your parents, to a stranger on the bus. Do it as many times as you can. If you want to feel more confident approaching the opposite sex, then just do it. Say 'hello', say 'good morning', say 'nice shoes'.

Take action and don't give up until you get the results you were aiming for. You may face setbacks, failures and rejections, but use them to learn from and to build more confidence.

Robyn's mind map looks like this:

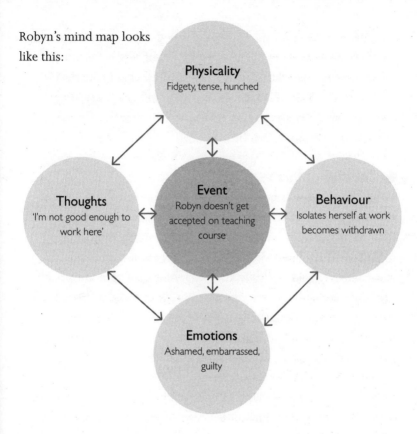

Physicality
Fidgety, tense, hunched

Thoughts
'I'm not good enough to work here'

Event
Robyn doesn't get accepted on teaching course

Behaviour
Isolates herself at work becomes withdrawn

Emotions
Ashamed, embarrassed, guilty

Instead of viewing her rejection from the course as a life-changing setback, Robyn could simply see it as an obstacle to be overcome. Yes, being rejected is rubbish, but she can use what she now knows to nail the application the next time around and she'll have an extra year to gain valuable experience. Viewing mistakes and difficulties as indelible representations of personal failures can rule your life. Robyn might leave her teaching assistant post and get another job that she doesn't find as fulfilling. She might never feel fully confident in her abilities again – and not just with teaching. She can let it cloud how she views herself in all aspects of life. Or she can use it to her advantage, apply again, get on the course and become a teacher. How you choose to view things will shape your life.

Ⓢ The rule of three

Make a list of three things you've always wanted to try that you can do in the next month. Find a way to do them and then go for it. Don't over-think it or over-research it – just get on with it. You can read about something until you go cross-eyed, but unless you actually try it you're never going to really know everything about it. You wouldn't just read a recipe book and consider yourself an excellent cook. You'd try the recipes out and practise a few times until you felt confident with them. Instead of seeing things in terms of success and failure, you need to channel your inner kid and use the learning to walk principle: if children never picked themselves up and tried again after falling over then we'd all still be shuffling around on our bums. Children don't know the concept of failing so they just leap in both feet first, which is exactly what you need to do.

+ Brainstorm a list of plausible things you'd like to try in the next month.
+ Pick three that are not too similar. One that's easy (i.e. 'give someone my number' or 'suggest drinks with colleagues after work'), one that's a little harder (i.e. 'chair a meeting at work', 'join a new

exercise class') and something that'll take more planning (i.e. 'enter a creative writing competition' or 'apply for an evening course').

+ Look into each of them and make a plan, so if one of your goals is to give someone your number organise a night out with some friends where you're likely to meet some single people.

+ Do it. Face the situation with enthusiasm and banish all thoughts of success or failure – see it as merely an experience, rather than something you'll be judged for. The success of this task is just to make yourself do it – how it turns out is irrelevant. So what if the person you give your number to turns round and tells you they're married? At least you tried.

+ Book it in again and have another go. Practise! It'll get easier each time you try.

Thoughts to take away

✓ Actually *doing* the things you're frightened of will increase your self-efficacy and therefore your confidence

✓ Perfection is a myth. Stop trying to live up to impossible ideals and instead focus on what you know you can do

✓ Embrace mistakes as part of the learning process. Pick yourself up when things don't work and try a different approach

6

Pride or Prejudice

Taking pride in your achievements is an essential part of building confidence. This chapter will teach you how to stop the prejudice you have against yourself and to start giving yourself the credit you deserve.

Appreciating the good things

A key part of building confidence is to take pride and pleasure in your achievements and to give yourself credit for what you've done well. You've spent far too long chastising yourself for your supposed failures and haven't paid nearly enough (if any) attention to the stuff that's been ticking along all fine and dandy.

You'll already be familiar with the myriad ways you can ignore both the good things that happen to you and the good things that you instigate: you'll discount positive compliments as fanciful, dismiss your achievements as flukes or down to luck and you'll dwell on criticism.

You're so used to ignoring your good points that you probably believe thinking about them at all is in some way arrogant or egotistical. Well, it's not. Recognising your positive attributes isn't in anyway conceited, it's actually really important. You need to know what your strengths are in order to put yourself in the best possible position to achieve what you want to. It's an integral part of building your self-esteem. You need to start showing yourself some goodwill.

Research studies suggest that there are different kinds of self-esteem. Some people may have a secure sense of self regardless of the situation, whereas others' self-worth might vary depending on their last accomplishment or who they are able to impress. When they are doing well they feel great, but when they come across any kind of setback they'll feel shame and self-doubt which results in an unhealthy vigilance around social status and performance. They have to keep comparing themselves to others to make sure they measure up and haven't fallen behind.

To feel truly confident you can't be constantly reliant on other people: you'll only ever feel as good as someone else makes you feel, which is a very precarious way to live. Approval from the people you look up to should always be an added bonus and never the basis for your valuations of self-worth.

So, instead of basing your self-belief on current feedback or how you're doing right now, you should have a broad view based on all your experiences, a sort of objective self-assessment of all your strengths and abilities. This kind of internal measure is not only much more secure, stable and realistic, but is just generally a nicer way to live.

⑤ Equal opportunities

Think of the last time you did something really well. It can be anything. Perhaps you got a good result, some excellent feedback, cooked a wonderful dinner or made a friend laugh. How did it make you feel? Now roughly estimate how much time you spent thinking about this. Ten minutes? Fifteen? Two?

Next, think of the last thing you did badly, incorrectly, or that didn't quite go as well as you wanted it to. Maybe you rushed a piece of work and had to correct it, or you argued with your partner and said something you regret. How did it make you feel? Now roughly estimate how much time you spent thinking about this. An hour? A day? A week?

Things have become so negatively skewed in your head that you probably found it quite difficult to think of anything you'd done well, automatically discounting little things like making a friend feel better as not important enough. This is nonsense. These things matter and are important reflections on your character.

We're willing to bet that you spent far longer thinking about the thing that went badly than you did about the thing that went well. It's not fair, but your negative biases will make all the things that you don't like about yourself – what you see as your faults – jump out and eclipse all your strengths. Because of this tendency, you're going to have to actively bring the good things kicking and screaming to the forefront of your mind.

Punish your prejudice

You are prejudiced against yourself. Nope, don't deny it. You are – it's a fact. Christine Padesky, co-founder of the Centre for Cognitive Therapy in California, states self-prejudice is a common symptom of LSE. Prejudice is an unfavourable opinion about something with basically zero evidence to back it up and it's an absolute monster to shift. For example, say someone is very prejudiced against women drivers. They believe all women drivers are inferior to men and any woman who's actually pretty handy behind the wheel is either an exception to the rule, only showed some skill once or is lying about how good they are. You could reel off a million stats or examples to show them how ridiculous this notion is, but they wouldn't care. They don't want to be proved wrong – and there's the rub.

You have to be open to hearing, digesting and believing new information that will counter your beliefs to get rid of a prejudice. So to get rid of self-prejudice you have to want to like yourself and believe in yourself. We're assuming you do otherwise you wouldn't be reading this book – so that's the first step completed. Now you just have to actively attend to all the information that disproves your prejudice and allow it to stick. Easy, eh?

Take a compliment (from others and from yourself)

To build your confidence you're going to have to start both giving yourself compliments and accepting them from others. It's all too easy to brush compliments off and dismiss them as people just being polite or friendly. Occasionally this might be true, but for the most part you earn the praise you receive.

Taking a compliment is an art. Other people want you to succeed and want you to feel good – now you just have to start believing them and believing in yourself. This doesn't mean you have to go around shouting about how great you are or wearing an 'I'm fantastic and I know it' badge. It's all about balance. By starting to acknowledge the positives you're just tipping the scales of self-evaluation back into balance.

The positive impact of acknowledging and accepting good things about yourself will have a knock-on effect on how you feel emotionally and physically and on what you do.

Example: A cookery lesson

Steph had been made redundant from her beloved job in marketing. She felt as if the rug had been pulled from beneath her feet. She was so devastated she hadn't even been able to look for other jobs. She just hid away at home and indulged her love of cooking. She started whipping up feasts and inviting all her friends round to eat as she always made too much.

⋯⋰ Soon it became a routine. Her mates would come round every Wednesday and Friday and she'd cook for them. Then one day her friend Jane called and asked if she could bring another friend, Lucie, round. She was going through a painful break-up and Jane had told her what a great cook Steph was and thought her food would cheer her up. Steph felt surprised, but secretly pleased. She knew she could cook well, but hadn't ever thought it was unusual or something worth noting. The fact Jane had told her friend was really flattering.

She cooked her favourite dish and seven people ended up piling round. Everyone raved about the food – particularly Lucie. She even said she knew of a market where they needed a food stall and suggested Steph should apply.

Steph had never considered her cooking as a talent to be proud of. It had always just been something she did – a pleasant hobby. Realising that other people valued her skill made her start valuing it too.

⑤ Loud and proud

Think of three things in your life that you're really proud of. They can be anything at all from any time. The only caveat is that you must have felt really confident in what you were doing and what you achieved. Forget about what others might consider as achievements, this is about what you felt proud of and what gave you a sense of satisfaction.

Steph's mind map looks like this:

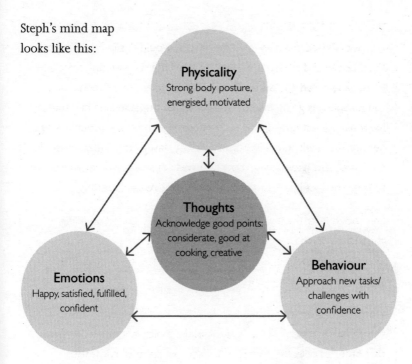

Physicality
Strong body posture, energised, motivated

Thoughts
Acknowledge good points: considerate, good at cooking, creative

Emotions
Happy, satisfied, fulfilled, confident

Behaviour
Approach new tasks/ challenges with confidence

Maybe your teacher chose your painting as her favourite at school, or you were interviewed on the news about your opinion on a topical story. Maybe you stepped in when you saw someone being bullied on the bus or gave your scarf to a homeless guy on the street. It doesn't matter whether you were alone or part of a team, they should just be things that made you feel great.

Write them down and then note underneath each one what you actually did, what you're most proud of about it and how it made you feel at the time.

If recalling great memories like that doesn't give you a burst of pride and confidence then you need to pick some other memories!

⑤ Your 'good bits' record

Now you're feeling slightly warmer towards yourself and grudgingly accepting that you might not be all bad, it's a great time to really focus on your good bits. Write as many positive things down about yourself that you can think of. It should include all your positive characteristics, strengths, talents and achievements. Write them down in your notebook or on your phone – somewhere you have easy access to so if more spring to mind you can include them quickly before you forget.

Take a couple of days over it. There's no rush. We want the list to be comprehensive. Just two or three things won't do. You may find yourself reluctant to do it at first, but remember – no one's going to see this list except you, so be totally honest. And don't worry, you're not being conceited.

Don't disregard any ideas too quickly – nothing is too small or insignificant – and don't let your inner judge pipe up and scoff at what you're doing. Your inner judge is an idiot: ignore it.

Remember: no one is their best selves 100 per cent of the time. We're all human. So if you'd generally consider yourself as being hardworking, but have had a tough couple of months and left the office early a few days in a row, don't discount 'hardworking' – write it down.

If you're struggling ask yourself the questions below for inspiration:

✦ What do I like about who I am?

✦ What am I good at?

✦ What positive character traits do I have?

✦ What skills and talents do I have?
✦ What do others say they like about me?
✦ What compliments have people given me?
✦ How have I overcome any challenges?
✦ What positive interactions have I had recently? Why were they positive?
✦ What attributes do I like in others that I might also possess?

After you've exhausted every possibility that you can think of ask a friend, partner or family member for their opinion. Other people are actually much better at judging us than we are ourselves. They'll no doubt think of some things you haven't. Yes, asking someone to list all your best bits might be intimidating so make sure it's someone you know well, so you can explain about this strategy and why you're doing it.

⑤ Backing up the positives

Making your list should have highlighted just how many qualities you have to be proud of, but because prejudice is a stubborn old mule we haven't finished yet. Go through your list and note down evidence that backs up each quality. Yes – each and every one. It's very easy just to write down words without taking them in: 'Oh yeah, I'm loyal.' Why are you? Prove it. By noting down specific examples each attribute will become real to you and you will have to accept it as a truth about yourself.

For instance:

✦ A good friend: I drove Sally to the airport at 5a.m. last week
✦ Determined: I called up the council four times until they fixed the

pothole in the road
+ Love music: I went to two gigs last month
+ Tolerant: I listened calmly to a bigoted old man on the train last week before (politely) telling him I thought his views were ridiculous
+ Organised: I planned a reunion dinner for all my college friends a month ago

Good-quality hunting

Here are some examples of personal qualities you might have:

Considerate, attentive, kind, loyal, reliable, clever, resourceful, hard-working, decisive, health-conscious, a good listener, dependable, keen reader, artistic, organised, determined, strong, funny, sporty, well-travelled, adventurous, compassionate, politically conscious, good general knowledge, creative, friendly, appreciative, diligent, discreet, enthusiastic, charitable, thoughtful, active, responsible, forgiving, gentle, good cook, helpful, house proud, a good friend, musical, outdoors person, determined, cultured, practical, fashion conscious, computer literate, punctual, understanding, open minded, hospitable, patient, orderly, persuasive, resourceful, sincere, thorough, sensitive, tolerant.

Thinking of examples for each of them will take time, but it's time well spent. It means you're actually giving your positive qualities the attention they deserve and you're forcing yourself to accept that they matter.

Goodwill hunting

You need to start recognising these positive attributes every day as they happen. Extend to your present self, the goodwill you've extended your past self.

✦ Write them down as and when they happen or you'll forget or disregard them later. It's all too easy to think, 'That actually wasn't a big deal' four hours after you ran after someone to hand back the wallet they'd dropped. It was a big deal, don't dismiss it. Make sure you find at least three every day:

Monday: Honest – owned up to making a mistake at work

Fun – made my sister laugh

Efficient – got my report in early

✦ Keep your list of positive qualities somewhere easily accessible so you can remind yourself of them and also use them for inspiration the next day.
✦ Give yourself credit for the small things. Don't wait for a massive fanfare to justify a pat on the back.
✦ You'll soon get used to noticing your good bits and find you can write down four or five easily. This really is progress – when you first picked up this book would you have been able to write down that

many good things about yourself every day?

✦ At the end of every day re-read what you have written and accept it. These things happened – you wrote them down, you can't deny them!

After one week flick back through the list. What would you think of someone else who possessed those skills and attributes? Do you think you'd like them? Do you think they should be confident? What if that person told you they had very low self-esteem? You'd think they were mad. Seeing your good bits in black and white like this should really hammer home that you can feel proud of yourself, you can cope with what life throws at you and you absolutely can make changes.

This is an on-going task which you should ensure fits seamlessly into your day until you feel more confident and your self-esteem is creeping up again. You've been collecting evidence that proves you're lacking for so long that it'll take a while for you to truly believe everything positive you write down so keep at it and soon it'll sink in.

Thoughts to take away

✓ Giving your good points as much focus (or hopefully more) than your supposedly 'bad' points is only fair and will hugely boost your confidence

✓ Stopping the prejudice you have against yourself will take time, but by focusing on evidence that disproves it you'll soon feel better about yourself

✓ Accepting compliments is an important part of generating self-belief

7

Walk the Walk

Carrying yourself confidently will make you feel more confident and vice versa. Looking self-assured, even if you're faking it, is an easy way to kick-start feelings of self-belief. This chapter is all about learning how to look and therefore feel the part.

Hold your head up high

If you've really embraced the strategies so far, hopefully you should be thinking and feeling far more confidently than you were just a few short weeks ago. And, if everything's ticking along as it should be, this will inevitably have affected how you present yourself physically and how you behave.

Humans interact through physical representations of their emotions and thoughts via non-verbal cues. We can all 'read' people through their expressions, ticks, posture, stance and how they act. While there are thousands of subtle cue variations, there are equally as many really obvious ones. If you're angry you might furrow your brow, grit your teeth, tense your jaw or clench your fists and if you're insecure you might hunch your shoulders, bite your nails, shake, or cross your arms. However, if you're feeling confident you'll probably have relaxed shoulders, be standing upright and have your head held high. You'll also act in more confident ways, e.g. by not crossing your arms, not shuffling when you walk, not staying silent or hiding under your desk.

Just as actually feeling confident will make you look confident, learning how to look confident (even if you're faking it) will make you feel more confident. It works both ways – a bit like how making yourself smile can cheer you up. A study published in the *European Journal of Social Psychology* found that subjects who sat up straight in their chairs instead of slouching were more confident about the things they were then asked to write down. They also discovered that posture builds a sense of strength and confidence in social situations too.

If you project an aura of capability people will respond to it, feeling as if they can trust you. Just as you would be wary of approaching someone who looked incredibly stressed or angry, you'll be encouraged about approaching someone who looks open, easy going and sure of themselves. You can become that person. If you look the part, you'll feel and act the part too.

Appearances can be deceiving

We carried out a survey and asked people what they believed would make someone appear either confident or unconfident. We have summarised the results below.

What does insecurity look and sound like?

Body language	Appearance	Actions
+ Poor eye contact	+ Scruffy	+ Weak handshake
+ Looking at the floor	+ Dark and/ or baggy clothes	+ Dithering / poor decision making / constantly changing their mind
+ Hunched	+ Make little effort	+ Don't stand up for themselves
+ Downturned mouth	+ Look uncomfortable	+ Constantly apologising
+ Twitching		+ Appear either needy or overly self-promoting
+ Rapid eye movement		+ Panicky and anxious

Characteristics	Speech	
		+ Scurry rather than walk/ rush around
+ Quiet	+ Stumble over words or stutter	+ Don't voice opinions
+ Shy	+ Hesitant speech patterns	+ Always back the loudest or most confident person in the room
+ Self-critical	+ Speak very quietly or quickly	+ Physically hide away or avoid people (either behind someone or near a corner or door)
+ Uncertain	+ Shout to try to get a reaction	
+ Brash		+ Keep coat on indoors, like they're ready for a quick escape
+ Self-promoting		

What does confidence look and sound like?

Body language	Appearance	Actions
+ Open (don't cross arms or put up 'body barriers') + Good eye contact + Stand up tall + Head and chin up + Shoulders back and relaxed	+ Well turned out + Look like they've made an effort + Look comfortable	+ Walk purposefully and assertively + Appear in control and not flustered + Decisive + Take action

Characteristics	Speech	
+ Honest + Self-assured + Not overly self-promoting + Seem knowledgeable + Happy in their own skin + Comfortable + Amenable + Friendly	+ Clear + Measured + Considered	

Example: The awkward audition

Mark was auditioning for a role in a car commercial. He didn't know why he'd bothered turning up though as there was no way he was going to get it. To prove to himself and everyone else how not-bothered he was he'd deliberately worn his oldest pair of jeans ⋯⋯

... and shabbiest trainers. The rest of the people auditioning were obviously way more experienced and better-looking than him, so why make an effort? He even recognised the guy from that award-winning BBC drama in the corner – great.

He felt it was inevitable that he'd be rejected for this role, making it the sixth consecutive 'no thanks' in two weeks. What was the point?

He took a quick peek at the script that the guy next to him was holding and his stomach lurched. It wasn't the same script that he had. He checked around – everyone was rehearsing from a different script. He showed the man sitting next to him the pages he had and he said he'd never seen them before. What the hell? How could this get any worse?

When it was his turn Mark shuffled into the room. His hands were shaking. 'I - I was given the wrong script,' he stuttered before crossing his arms over his chest defensively. 'Well, don't panic,' one of the three people sitting behind the intimidatingly large desk in front of him said. 'We'll just give you the right one and you can try your best.'

Mark snatched up the new lines and delivered the worst performance of his life. Actually, the worst performance of anyone's life. When he was finished he stomped out angrily without even saying thanks or goodbye.

Mark's mind map looks like this:

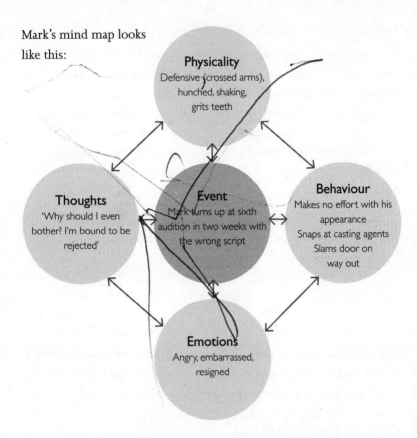

Physicality
Defensive (crossed arms), hunched, shaking, grits teeth

Thoughts
'Why should I even bother? I'm bound to be rejected'

Event
Mark turns up at sixth audition in two weeks with the wrong script

Behaviour
Makes no effort with his appearance
Snaps at casting agents
Slams door on way out

Emotions
Angry, embarrassed, resigned

It was perhaps inevitable that Mark's confidence had taken a nose-dive after so many rejections, however, appearing confident even if you're faking it is great way of tricking yourself into feeling more confident.

By choosing not to take any care with how he dressed Mark was already in a 'screw you' defensive mindset. When he then discovered he'd got the wrong script his body language, speech and behaviour all determined to make him appear unapproachable, unconfident and angry which consequently made him feel unapproachable, unconfident and angry. It became a self-fulfilling prophecy.

Things would have been so different if he'd tried to at least look confident. If he'd taken care over what he wore he would have felt more comfortable in himself and in the appearance he was projecting, making him less likely to dismiss his chances on the grounds of what other people looked like. His thoughts would then have been far calmer when he realised he had the wrong script and he could march assertively into the audition room, explain the situation and ask if he could act the part with the script he had to show them what he could do with lines he was familiar with. He could then suggest reading from the script he hadn't seen before to prove he was amenable, capable and unflustered by change. The casting agents would be more likely to agree to this plan when faced with a laid-back confident, non-confrontational guy then they would with a shaking ball of fury. If Mark had just been more aware of his non-verbal cues his mind map could have looked like the one on page 106.

⑤ Your 'chin up' mind map

Think of a recent time when you felt really insecure and fill out a mind map to show what happened, how you felt emotionally, what you were thinking, how it made you act, and what effect it had on you physically.

Next, fill out another one about a time when you felt really confident.

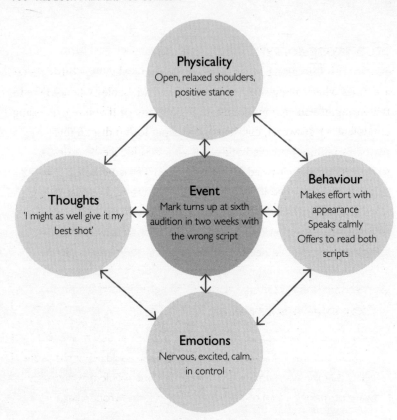

When you've finished, compare the two mind maps. Can you see the difference projecting an aura of confidence – physically and behaviourally – will have on how you feel and think? And, it won't only affect how you perceive yourself it'll affect how others perceive you too. Research has found that we form our initial impressions of other people in the first five seconds of meeting them. Making changes to how you carry yourself is a really simple way to look, feel and act more confident.

Stop saying sorry

People with LSE can find themselves apologising a lot. Obviously there are times when saying sorry is necessary and advisable (when you're in the wrong, if you've done something you regret or if you're expressing condolences). However, constant apologising for no discernible reason can dilute your credibility and your confidence. Your desire to apologise will be caused by NATs such as, 'I'm ridiculous', 'I'm ruining this' or 'I need to excuse myself'. You can end up just saying sorry for being you, which means you're projecting yourself as inferior to whoever you're speaking to and this will translate itself into an apologetic demeanour because you'll probably look embarrassed.

Example: A sorry story

Anna was constantly apologising and putting herself down. She had a great job and was in a stable relationship, but she could never shake the feeling that she was somehow in the wrong. She would be constantly aware of making a fool of herself or of saying the wrong thing.

Someone had once told her she could kill a conversation at twenty paces and she'd never forgotten it. She was terrified of interrupting people or just generally being annoying. NATs such as 'You're so irritating', 'You always ruin jokes' and 'Everyone thinks you're embarrassing' were allowed to whizz through her head whenever they fancied. While she didn't want people to think her constant apologising was a ruse to get reassurance, that's actually exactly ⋯⋅

⋯⋮ what it was. She ended up physically shrinking from conversations, hiding away in the background and never putting her opinion across.

Her friend suggested that before she next opened her mouth to say sorry she take a moment to really think about whether she needed to. Had she done something wrong? Was she dishing out a condolence? If not then she shouldn't say it!

Anna took her advice and the next time she was about to apologise when someone said they couldn't attend her dinner party she stopped herself. The fact they couldn't make it wasn't her fault, was it? So she said, 'Ah, never mind. That's a shame. Next time,' instead, and felt a tiny weight of guilt and responsibility lift from her shoulders.

⑤ Sorry dos and don'ts

+ Do apologise if you've done something wrong, hurt someone's feelings or want to make amends.
+ Do apologise if you're expressing condolences.
+ Don't apologise for being right. When you're right, you're right and there's no need to soften the blow with a sheepish, 'sorry'. You can still sound considerate without apologising.
+ Don't apologise for your opinion. 'I'm sorry, but I was thinking …' Why should you be sorry for thinking? No one else is sorry for their opinion so why should you be for yours? By saying sorry you are just undermining your point of view.

✦ Don't apologise for asking for help. Asking for help isn't an imposition, but by constantly saying sorry you're making whatever you need seem a bigger burden then it really is. You should make it positive, i.e. 'Could you possibly assist me with X because you're really good at it?'

Dressing to impress (yourself)

Whatever you think about clothes or style how you choose to dress is a reflection of how you view yourself and how you want other people to view you. It doesn't matter whether you care about the latest trends or not, what you choose to wear to work or to socialise in is one of the most blatant non-verbal cues you can give.

Everyone's different and there's no right or wrong way to dress. The key is to feel comfortable in what you wear, whatever that is. If you suffer from LSE feeling good about what you're wearing will make you feel more confident. Dressing suitably for an occasion is such an easy way to avoid feeling out of place or embarrassed. If you're an insecure person then wearing jeans and trainers to a black-tie event or a suit to a laid-back gig is a guaranteed way of racking up your panic levels.

If you have a tendency to hide away under baggy clothes, but know you're only doing it because you don't want to draw attention to yourself then consider changing things a bit. Whatever your shape or size there will be clothes to suit you and make you feel better. Consider visiting a personal shopper (many shops and department stores offer this as a free service) or asking a friend to go with you to try on things that take you slightly out of your comfort zone.

Taking risks with your clothes will make you feel brave. You don't have to go crazy and start wearing leather trousers underneath a ra-ra skirt if that's not your thing, but just adding a bit of colour or pattern to your wardrobe if you usually stick to dark hues will make you feel good because you've done something different.

In order of appearance

Always remember that other people feel insecure too. Now that you're more aware of these non-verbal cues you'll be able to pick them out in other people and assess their effect from an outsider's perspective. This will make you realise that some things you may have previously taken personally and believed were a reflection on you are actually just examples of other people's nerves. For example, if Jake from accounts can never look you in the eye and seems to avoid you, it's almost definitely not because he doesn't like you, but because he's shy and suffers from the same fears you do.

People are actually pretty self-involved on the whole. We never expend the same level of detail or scrutiny on others as we do on ourselves. When you flick through photographs chances are you'll spend longer analysing the pictures you appear in than you do the ones of other people. People are far more judgemental about what they look like than they are about anyone else. Keep this in mind if you feel intimidated by making changes.

Comparison crisis

Comparing ourselves to other people is natural. The survival-of-the-fittest shtick that our cave-dwelling ancestors lived by is still alive and well. It's how people measure success and can drive us to succeed. However, when you're feeling insecure you're far more likely to compare yourself negatively to others and constantly find yourself lacking. This will just exacerbate your self-doubt and might even trigger an inferiority complex.

Unfortunately, in today's twenty-four hour society we're constantly bombarded by images of what pop culture deems 'aspirational'. This changes week by week, but the messages can stick with us for life. When you suffer from LSE you can find opportunities for self-recrimination everywhere: in adverts, in television programmes, on celebrity gossip sites, etc. But you can choose how you process this information and what you do with it. You know realistically and logically that the appearance of people in adverts and movies doesn't bear much resemblance to how they look in real life – minus the make-up artists, personal trainers and on-call sushi chefs. It's a mirage.

Next time you catch yourself comparing yourself negatively to someone, stop and find a balanced view. Are you being fair on yourself and do you know the full story? Yes, Emma on the front desk always looks impeccable, but she would actually love your job. Yes, your friend Nick is hilariously witty and always ⋯⋮⋅

> ⋯⋰> appears so confident, but you know he's actually very nervous
> around new people. We're not saying you should deliberately look
> for people's bad bits, just make sure you're being fair on yourself
> before hoisting them up on a pedestal.

⑤ Keeping up appearances

Start incorporating confident body language and behaviour into
your day-to-day life. It's so simple – whenever you notice that you're
slouching, crossing your arms, fidgeting or edging towards a door
… stop. Drop your shoulders and push them back, raise your chin,
uncross your arms and stand up tall. Remember to make eye contact
and smile. Speak clearly and don't rush. Consider what you wear and
whether you're willing to change things a bit. If you're always in jeans
and trainers maybe buy some smarter shoes or invest in a skirt. Or if
you're always suited and booted try some jeans instead.

    While these changes may be considerable to you, other people
will have no idea they're unusual or scary. They're not going to get a
megaphone and announce to the whole office, 'Carly's wearing a skirt
for the first time in fifteen years! Everybody stare at it!' They'll just say,
'nice skirt', and you'll feel great. If you need some added motivation,
use the imagery strategy from Chapter 4 to imagine the best version
of you. Picture how you stand, move and even speak. Then go and
recreate that version in reality.

Thoughts to take away

✓ Making small changes to your body language will make huge differences to how others view you and, most importantly, how you view yourself

✓ Appearing more confident will make you feel more confident and vice versa

✓ How you dress, carry yourself physically and how you act can all project an aura of confidence

8

Social Benefits

Both socialising and interacting with people professionally can be incredibly intimidating when you feel unsure of yourself. This chapter is all about how to relax and have faith that you really are good company.

Social confidence

When you lack confidence, social situations can be bone-chilling. Something that should be fun and laid-back becomes something to dread and avoid at all costs. And this isn't just in personal contexts, but professional ones too. Fear of being judged by others or of not living up to the ridiculous standards of behaviour you have set up in your head can mean you'll already feel like a failure before you've even arrived. The more you focus on yourself, the harder it becomes to engage with other people and you'll end up acting exactly as you feared – shy, stand-offish, unengaged and uninterested.

You're so anxious about appearing anxious, that any semblance of confidence you had will run away screaming in terror.

Putting yourself under this amount of pressure means you're going to be painfully aware of yourself at the event. Panicking about how you come across will make you hyper-conscious of how you appear and of how other people are responding to you, scuppering any chances you had of looking relaxed and calm.

Feeling this fraught will also impact on your behaviour. You might rehearse what you're going to say beforehand which can make your conversation seem somewhat formal and stilted. You'll inevitably also feel wrong-footed when the chat takes a turn that you did not foresee. Or you might mask your insecurity behind bravado and actually come across as quite rude and bolshy. You'll also be less engaged with the people you're with, which can give the impression that you don't care about what they have to say.

The three bugbears of socialising

People who find social situations difficult often believe they have to
behave in certain ways to 'fit in' or they won't have a good time.
Below are the three most common socialising bugbears that will
haunt LSE sufferers:

1 Excessively high standards: 'I must sound funny, clever, witty and
   charming at all times. I must always have something interesting to
   say and I must never admit to not knowing what someone is
   talking about.'

2 Performance anxiety: 'I cannot show any sign of weakness (I cannot
   look nervous or anxious) or people will think I'm odd or stupid
   and I can't be too quiet or people will think I'm boring.'

3 Negative self-beliefs: 'I cannot let anyone think that I'm a fake or
   they'll guess that I'm actually weird, boring and not like them.'

Example: Oliver's stand-up routine

Oliver was so nervous about meeting his girlfriend's friends for the
first time that he spent fifteen minutes psyching himself up in the
bathroom mirror when they arrived at the bar. 'Don't be ⋯

⋯⋮⋅ nervous,' he ordered herself. 'Tell that joke you heard the other day – they'll love it.'

He went out and joined the group. Everyone seemed friendly, but twenty minutes quickly slipped by and he realised he still hadn't really contributed to the conversation or made his mark. He'd just said 'yes' here and there. 'I'm coming across badly,' he thought. 'They're all going to think I'm boring.' He interrupted the guy who was speaking with a witty comment. Everyone laughed. He then changed the subject and told a funny story he knew would go down well. It did. He was on a roll! He quickly told another … and another … and then demanded another drink from whoever was due to buy the next round.

He didn't even realise he hadn't given anyone else a chance to talk and when they did squeeze in a few comments he was so busy preparing the next thing he was going to say, he didn't listen.

Oliver's mind map looks like the one on the opposite page.

Social self-confidence is as much about feeling relaxed with other people as feeling relaxed with yourself, which means you can't be scared to make mistakes. Being nervous before meeting your partner's friends for the first time is completely normal and the people you're meeting would know that. They wouldn't mind if you were quiet for a bit and they wouldn't care if you told a rubbish joke. What they would mind is being interrupted and ignored.

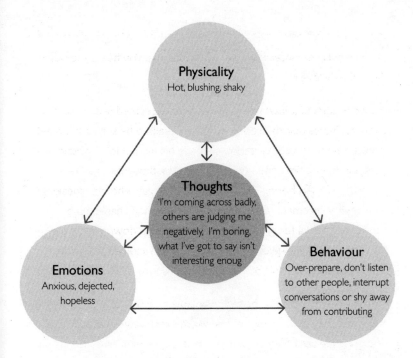

Physicality
Hot, blushing, shaky

Thoughts
'I'm coming across badly, others are judging me negatively, I'm boring, what I've got to say isn't interesting enoug

Behaviour
Over-prepare, don't listen to other people, interrupt conversations or shy away from contributing

Emotions
Anxious, dejected, hopeless

Getting out of your head

If you're out with other people, but stuck in your own head you might as well not be there at all. You're so busy planning how not to mess up and listening to your own negative self-commentary, that you're actually messing up by not paying attention or listening to whoever you're with. How can you contribute if you have no idea what's going on? It's a vicious circle.

By stepping out of your head and concentrating on what's going on around you, you'll feel more confident about socialising. It's genuinely that simple.

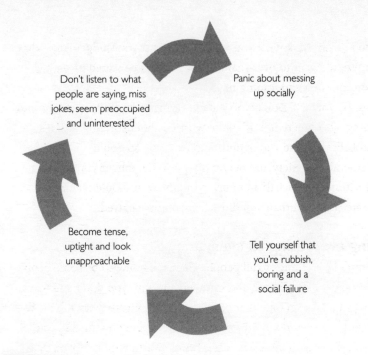

Don't listen to what people are saying, miss jokes, seem preoccupied and uninterested

Panic about messing up socially

Become tense, uptight and look unapproachable

Tell yourself that you're rubbish, boring and a social failure

Ⓢ Listen up

The next time you're in a social situation whenever you catch yourself thinking about how you might be coming across, what you should say next, whether people think you're boring or whether you've said enough funny stuff, stop and follow these rules:

+ Really focus on what the person you're with is saying. Stop thinking about yourself and think about them.

+ Treat them as you would like to be treated (yes, that old chestnut). Just as you're worried about appearing boring, no doubt they will be too and if you're staring at the floor or out of the window they'll feel anxious.

+ Don't over-think what you want to say. Trust your judgement. While you don't want to over-share or boast, don't be scared of stating your opinion and joining in.
+ Just be yourself. Don't worry about trying to be really clever or into things that you're not. If you're worried about seeming fake it's probably because you're putting on an act – so don't.
+ Remember, anxiety and nerves disappear the longer you stay in a situation so after half an hour or an hour you should feel much more confident than you did when you first arrived.

Being everything to everyone

You can't be all things to all people. There are going to be some people who you get on well with and some people who you don't and that's not a bad reflection on either you or them. It's just the way life is. We have more in common with certain people and find them easier to be around. Being honest will make people warm to you. If you try to be everyone's best pal you'll spread yourself too thin and will end up giving lots of people not enough time, rather than a few people lots of time. Also, keeping up an act like this will undermine your self-belief as you'll start questioning who you really are and who you should be. Other people might start questioning it too, because only saying what you think people want to hear will appear disingenuous. Be confident in your own opinion.

What you think and what you say does have value and the sooner you accept that the sooner you'll relax and start having a good time with people you genuinely like.

The drink and drugs debate

Alcohol and recreational drugs can seem like a quick fix when you're nervous or insecure. They loosen the tongue and give you a seemingly much needed boost for a few hours, before the inevitable crash/ guilty hangover.

For someone who lacks confidence drink and drugs only exacerbate the problems and the self-guilt cycle. Your behaviour is exaggerated – you can become a turbo-charged version of yourself – and you'll start to believe that they are the reason for your good time so you have more – and more. Soon you'll believe that drink or drugs are the only way you can feel good about yourself which can inevitably lead to dependency as they become the foundation of your self-belief. If this rings a bell with you lay off the booze and stop taking drugs for the next few weeks while you're working through this book. You need to prove to yourself that you can have a good time without them which will bolster your self-esteem.

⑤ Eavesdropping

The next time you're out at a party or in a pub listen (subtly) into some other people's conversations. Casually try to overhear what's being said. Nine times out of ten, we bet that people are chatting about totally mundane everyday things. When you're worried about not being funny, clever or interesting enough, it's very easy to assume that everyone else is having The Best Conversation of All Time. There are some people who are naturally gifted storytellers, who can make people roar with laughter and who can spark conversation with anyone and everyone. While that is of course brilliant, it's also rare. Most people are just having a non-pressurised chat, probably about the weather, what's on TV or what they're planning to do that weekend. Listening in and hearing this will be a real wake-up call. Not everyone's conversations are award-winning comedy gold or air-punching political debates so stop kicking yourself for being normal!

Talk is cheap

Snooping on other folks' conversations should have made you feel much less pressured to produce hilarious anecdotes on tap. It should also have reassured you that people are all much of a muchness. Everyone wants to be liked and to be thought interesting. Therefore if you show interest in other people, they'll show an interest in you – politeness goes a long way when socialising. To convince your negatively skewed brain of this though you need to find some proof.

⑤ Become a chatterbox

One of the best ways to overcome a fear of talking in public or at social occasions is to get into a habit of speaking up and talking to strangers. Over the next week we want you to turn into a chatterbox.

1 Start small. Say 'hello or 'good morning' to someone every day – either a stranger or an acquaintance. It can be anyone: a kid in a shop, the bus driver, the postman or your neighbours. Just say it with a smile. Don't worry if they return the greeting or not. Don't over-think it, just get into the habit of doing it.

2 When you're comfortable with this, extend your speaking mission to two people and increase the length of your conversations to 'Hello. All right?' You'll be surprised by how chuffed people will be that someone's showing an interest in them.

Social comparison crisis

In Chapter 7 we mentioned how damaging it can be to compare ourselves physically to other people. The same rules apply when it comes to comparing yourself socially.

You'll deliberately pick out your worst bits and compare them to other people's best bits. You'll think, 'Eva is so much funnier than me, I can never make people laugh like that,' rather than, 'Eva really makes me laugh.' Eva's ability to make people laugh is no reflection on you. She hasn't sucked up all the funniness in the room. Just because she's witty doesn't mean you're not.

Rather than seeing other people's good bits as things you are lacking, use them as inspiration, e.g. 'Eva's funny and she seems to like me which makes me feel good' or 'Eva doesn't care whether people like her jokes or not so maybe I shouldn't care either?' Or, better yet, don't compare yourself at all. Everyone's different and there are no doubt things you do, have or say that other people admire too. Just be yourself and enjoy other people for who and what they are.

3 Touch base with a friend you haven't spoken to in a while. Either phone them or meet up face-to-face – but make sure you talk to them. Nowadays it's all too easy for relationships to move online and people we used to know well are relegated solely to Facebook or email 'friends'. You can lose the closeness of conversation. You'll be so used to considering what message you're going to write back that all chatty spontaneity is lost. It's also easy to misread tone in an online message, which can cause lots of confidence issues. Speaking to people will reassert that personal connection.

Public speaking paranoia

Whether you have to make a presentation at work or a speech at a wedding, public speaking can reduce the most confident person to a bag of nerves. You can feel exposed and your fear will manifest itself through dire assumptions about the audience's intentions: 'That idiot in the paisley jumper is just waiting for me to fall off the stage.' This is total nonsense of course, but when you're in that mindset it's hard to get out of.

Key facts to remember when speaking in front of an audience:

✦ Everyone wants you to do well. No one will be rooting for you to fail. People are, on the whole, pretty reasonable and everyone will be sympathetic to your nerves.

✦ No one will be paying lots of attention to what you look like. (No offence.) People will want to be interested in what you're saying; no one wants to be bored so they're not going to be analysing what you've done with your hair, they're going to be listening.

✦ If you make a mistake, who cares? When you last heard a talk did you dwell on that moment when the speaker tripped over a word or did you just forget it?

Being good at speaking in public is all about practice and preparation. Know your content inside and out, so you feel totally comfortable with what you have to get across. However, be careful not to over-prepare or you'll sound like a robot – a robot that can't respond to questions or adapt their script to suit the audience.

⑤ Battling public-speaking terrors

It doesn't matter whether you're speaking in front of one person or one thousand people, speaking slowly, clearly and concisely will keep everyone engaged – and the best way to do that is to practise. Start by speaking up in group discussions to get over your fear of 'messing up' in some way. The more practice you get at just chatting in front of people the more you'll realise that stumbling over a word here or there doesn't matter.

When you do have to make a speech consider trying the following:

✦ Imagine yourself talking to good friends. How would you present this topic to them and what would you say? You should talk to a large group of people as if they're just an extended group of your mates.

✦ Write down the main points you want to get across. Make sure you're really familiar with the topic and sure of the angle you're going to take.

✦ Write down some key lines in bold on a series of cue cards. You'll need to look up at the audience and the highlighted lines will jump out at you when you look back down so you won't lose your place.

+ Practise by reading slowly and clearly out loud. Some phrases and words are easy to read, but much harder to say so you need to be confident with your enunciation.
+ Try not to refer too much to your notes so you can adapt what you're saying to suit and engage the audience. Practise looking up after every third sentence. You can carry on speaking or you can just pause.
+ Don't worry about pausing. In your head the pauses will seem much longer than they are in reality so take your time.
+ Enthusiasm is contagious. If you are passionate about what you're saying other people will be too. If you're droning on in a monotone you could say, 'and then I dodged a bullet and rescued the President' and no one would bat an eyelid.
+ Be flexible with what you say. There's no way a speech can be relaxed and enjoyable if you have to say things in a certain way. Don't be scared to add a little line here or there. When you're too strict in following lines and you veer off course it can be hard to find your way back
+ Don't be scared of making mistakes. If you do lose your place just say, 'Excuse me a moment, I'm lost!' People are on your side. They'll laugh politely and wait. It's not a big deal.

Keeping it real

You have to accept that how you feel about something isn't necessarily how others feel or a good reflection of how things really are. For example, you may think you're really boring and not good company, but other people find you really engaging and interesting. You may think you're a terrible public speaker, but your boss thinks you're really calm, concise and have a knack for getting difficult people on side. You're not a mind-reader so projecting your thoughts onto others is unfair on both them and you.

⑤ A truth record

Next time you're out socialising or making a presentation at work ask someone to record you. Okay, so that may sound weird when you're in the pub, but most phones have a video function nowadays and it shouldn't be hard to ask a friend to catch a few minutes of the night here and there. You can either explain to them what you're doing and why or be cryptic about it – say you just want to see how everyone gets on and how the night went.

✦ Before you watch the clip consider how well you think the night or speech went and how you came across. Answer the questions below with marks out of ten (0 = terrible/ terribly/ not at all, 10 = brilliant/ brilliantly/ very):

    How confident did you appear?
    How did other people respond to you?
    How nervous did you look?

✦ Watch the clip as if you are watching a stranger – be open and as unbiased as possible. Ensure that you are basing your judgements on what you're actually seeing and hearing rather than on how you know you felt at the time. Now, re-rate how you did using the same questions you previously answered before watching the clip.

Typically how you think you come across bears no resemblance to reality. Hopefully your ratings after having actually watched the clip were much more positive than they were before you'd seen it. This should prove that how you picture yourself in your head, how you feel about yourself and how you imagine yourself coming across isn't a true reflection of what's actually happening. No one knows your insecurities but you.

Next time you're feeling anxious remind yourself of this exercise and that your worst-case imaginings are way off base. You can always use the imagery exercise in Chapter 4 to help with this, picturing how the best version of you would appear, act or perform a speech and then copy everything they did when you do it for real.

Thoughts to take away

✓ You don't have to be a stand-up comedian or an intellectual genius to be good company

✓ Socialising is all about listening and being yourself. It's ridiculously easy when you think of it that way

✓ Feeling anxious and making mistakes occasionally is normal – no one's going to notice or care

9

A Token of
Your Esteem

This chapter is all about how to treat yourself well, trust your instincts and put everything you've learned so far into practice. You can make changes and you can *choose* how you want to live.

Treating yourself well

As you'll no doubt be aware by now confidence comes in all different shapes and sizes. Looking after yourself and your best interests is a key part of self-belief. You have to learn to trust your judgement and your decision-making capabilities. This means that if you feel you're doing a good job then you probably are, just as if you feel you're being taken advantage of or treated badly then you probably are. Self-esteem isn't just about having faith in yourself to do well, it's also about knowing how to learn from your mistakes, trusting your instincts and asking for help when you need it.

You need to learn how to treat yourself properly. You have been denying yourself some basic rights for far too long: the right to be right, the right to screw up occasionally, the right to stand up for yourself, and the right to relax and have some fun. All of these things are fundamental to living a fulfilled life and you owe yourself that.

Here, we look at areas of your life that you might have avoided dealing with because you didn't trust your gut-reactions or ability to make good decisions. It covers everything from relationships, accepting advice and transferring the confidence you feel in some areas of your life to other parts that might need it.

Toxic relationships

When you're trying something new it's important to have support. Studies have demonstrated that having a network of supportive relationships promotes psychological well-being, providing you with a sense of self-worth and security. Knowing you have people around you who won't judge you and who care about you no matter what, isn't something you should take for granted; it's a great self-esteem booster.

The good news is that while you can't choose your family you can choose your friends and partners. You should nurture the friendships and relationships that are important in your life … just like you should be wary of the ones that aren't.

Just because you used to share a paddling pool with Janet when you were babies doesn't mean you have to put up with her constantly criticising you and making you feel miserable now. And just because you've been with Simon for years doesn't mean you have to accept his bullying ways. People who compromise your confidence aren't really friends and definitely aren't good boyfriends/ girlfriends or husbands/ wives. You need to become aware of toxic relationships in your life and feel confident enough not to continually find excuses for them. You can always find an excuse for someone's behaviour if you look hard enough, but should you have to?

Toxic relationships at work can be very difficult to deal with as you can't choose to cut your boss or your colleague out of your life or necessarily give them a piece of your mind. Constantly being undermined, overlooked or just feeling you have nowhere to turn can really affect your self-esteem. But don't worry, there are proactive things you can do to deal with toxic relationships both at home and work.

⑤ Quarantining toxic relationships

If someone is making you unhappy and it's really affecting your life then you have to deal with it. Avoiding the issue or putting off facing up to it will only make it seem bigger and more insurmountable. Also, the things that annoy you or upset you about this person will just become more annoying and more upsetting the longer it goes on making it more likely that one day you'll just explode and say something you regret.

Dealing with a toxic friend:

+ Talk to them about it. Organise a time to speak face to face. And yes, it does have to be face to face because you can't read tone in an email so things can be misconstrued.
+ Explain calmly why you feel upset by their behaviour and listen to what they've got to say. Try not to be confrontational.
+ Leave it up to them to make the next move. The truth is you are probably better off without them in your life, as hard as that is to hear. Unless they acknowledge what they've been doing, then it's not going to stop. You don't have to accept their bad behaviour.
+ If they want to talk, hear them out. Maybe they have some home truths to tell you too. You can then decide whether you want to keep them in your life and either do or don't. It's up to you.
+ If they don't accept any responsibility for their actions then cut them out and move on. A toxic friend is no friend at all.

Dealing with a toxic colleague:

+ Ask another colleague for their opinion. Someone you get on with who will give you an unbiased view. It's very hard to be objective when you feel under attack, so hearing another opinion might shed some light on an emotional situation.
+ Ask for a meeting with the toxic colleague and speak to them about where your relationship is going wrong. Again, don't be

confrontational or blame them (even if it's totally their fault).
Remain neutral, saying things like, 'I feel as if we're not seeing eye
to eye on a few things, is there anything we can do to sort this out?'
Keep saying 'we' rather than 'you'.

+ If nothing changes, have a meeting with your superior and ask
for their help. Say you're not sure where to go from here, but that
something has to be done.

+ If nothing improves or no one is taking you seriously and you've
gone as high as you can then consider leaving. As dramatic as that
sounds your emotional health is too important to risk for a job. You
will start questioning your own abilities and this will spiral into
your personal life too. It's not worth it.

Know when to ask for help

We've highlighted the importance of asking for help at several stages of
this book and we're going to do it again, because once you understand
that asking for and accepting help isn't a weakness you'll be well on
your way to feeling much more confident.

Everyone is good at some things and not so good at others. If
someone criticises you, you should see it as an opportunity to improve.
If someone does something better than you, you should see it as
an opportunity to learn. If you fall short, you should know you can
do better next time. If you feel embarrassed then laugh at yourself.
Understanding that there are some things you don't know is essential
for being a well-rounded person.

Being a know-it-all can get you into trouble. For example, if you
blag your way through a conversation about Iranian politics with your

boss one day you might find yourself questioned on the subject during the next presentation to the CEO, leaving you stuttering and mumbling like a complete fool.

Confidence is all about knowing when to admit you don't know. People who project an aura of capability are those who you trust to do the right thing and sometimes the right thing is to admit when you're out of your depth. We often lose sight of the big picture when we get caught up in our own microscopic view of things. Asking for help won't make you a burden and doesn't mean you're inadequate, weak or inferior. It actually shows a lot of courage.

The reality is that asking for help doesn't reflect anything about your character – it simply means that you need help with a specific situation. Think back to the times you've been asked for help. Did you think the person who asked you was stupid or ridiculous? We doubt it. In fact, it most probably made you feel good about yourself. Don't weigh your worth on what you don't know or can't do, weigh it on your willingness and capacity to learn.

⑤ Asking for advice and assistance

To get you into the habit of requesting help and so you can see first-hand how much people love being asked, we want you to ask someone for assistance every day next week. It can be anything from asking a stranger for directions to asking a friend for their advice on a work matter.

This exercise will definitely take some getting used to if you're someone who would rather wander around lost for hours than ask for directions or who would rather blunder on with a project than admit they're stuck. The more you practise asking, the more comfortable it will feel. You'll realise that no one resents being asked – in fact 99.9 per cent of people will absolutely love it, they'll feel flattered. Getting someone's help on really important things (e.g. relationship issues or work troubles) will make you feel so much better. You won't have to cope with everything on your own and getting someone else's perspective will give you some much needed distance from the problem.

Look on the bright side

Most of us will feel more confident in some areas of life than in others. For example, you may be pretty confident in your relationship, but not at work. You and your partner have a solid partnership and have been very happy for years, so at home you feel good about yourself. However at work you constantly doubt yourself and your abilities. It's like having two separate lives. The different roles we play demand different things from us and our measures for success vary dramatically depending on what we believe is being asked of us. The trick is to transfer the confidence you feel in one area into the others where you feel less sure of yourself.

⑤ Crossing confidence borders

A simple way to up your confidence levels in the areas where they could use a boost is to channel the feeling of self-assurance you have when you're feeling good about yourself. Using the example above for instance, when you're at work and feeling crappy, take five minutes, relax and remember your home life. Picture yourself when you're at your most comfortable and recall what your partner says to you that makes you feel secure – really let yourself feel that confidence and security. Remember that feeling when you next need an injection of confidence. You could even bring a memento from home to work – say a photograph – and look at it whenever you need a lift.

Accepting yourself

We've said a couple of times that you should 'be yourself'. We understand though that when you've been suffering from LSE for ages it can be hard to know where 'you' start and the person you've been trying to be, ends. Learning who you are and who you want to be won't happen overnight, but a good starting point is to focus on your likes and dislikes and what you're good at. Work from there. Rather than thinking about the things you can't control, concentrate on those you can. As a part of gaining confidence it's important to view your flaws as an integral aspect of being human rather than as proof that you are lacking.

Learning to accept yourself for who you are, will make you more comfortable in your own skin. You'll appear more authentic to yourself and to everyone else, and all of the insecurities that were associated with your quest to be someone you're not, will disappear.

A big part of acceptance is recognising that no matter how talented or capable you are, you cannot predict or control everything that happens in your life. Even confident people lose jobs, relationships and sometimes their health. True confidence comes from acknowledging this, but knowing that if the worst does happen you'll find a way to cope with it.

Do what you want

A horrible symptom of LSE is losing interest in looking after yourself
– because you don't deserve it, right? Withdrawing from life, engaging
in fewer activities and never treating yourself are natural when you feel
you're terrible company or not worth it. Unfortunately though you're
removing the things that naturally lifted your mood and made you feel
good about yourself.

You do deserve to have fun, to look good and to enjoy yourself. You
deserve to be treated well and to be proud of your accomplishments.
If you want other people to believe in you and to give you some
attention, you have to start believing in yourself and giving yourself
attention. A simple way to do this is to be good to yourself, treat
yourself kindly and make yourself a priority. Replace, 'I don't have
time' with 'I'll try to fit it in'. If you believe you're worth it, other
people will too.

Treating yourself well may also mean giving yourself permission
to say no and to stop doing things that make you feel bad (like
ditching toxic friends). If you don't like playing football, but always
felt pressured to, then stop. If you always go to the same hideous pub
which you hate with your friends then suggest going somewhere
else. If you are bored with your long hair then cut it. You need to take
control of your life and feel confident in your own decisions.

Increasing the amount of enjoyment and pleasure in your week will
automatically lift your mood and make you feel better about yourself
and your life. It's difficult to wake up in the morning faced with only
what you have to do or need to do. As well as making decisions for
you, you need to start having some fun.

⑤ Compulsory fun

Yes, we're ordering you to have some fun. Schedule in something you like or enjoy into every single day of next week. Write it in your diary in advance so it's 'official' and you're less likely to skip it. Having something to look forward to will increase your motivation and make you feel more able to cope with the harder, less exciting stuff you have to do.

Below are some ideas to get you started:

+ Give yourself a lie in, try out a new class or watch your favourite TV programme.
+ Take time out during the day to relax. Leave your desk for lunch and sit outside, listen to some music, go to a great coffee shop, read a magazine.
+ Do some exercise. Physical fitness has a huge effect on self-confidence. By working out you'll feel more energized and gain a sense of accomplishment.
+ Try something new that you've always wanted to do, e.g. join a life-drawing class or a netball team.
+ Buy some new clothes that make you feel good about yourself.
+ Eat well. Eating healthily will reduce the guilt associated with over- or under-eating and bingeing. Also by avoiding junk food, you're avoiding any sugar crashes.
+ Book in time to see friends and family.

Thoughts to take away

✓ Accepting yourself for who you are – flaws and all – will make you feel more confident

✓ Knowing when to ask for help and seek advice is a strength not a weakness

✓ Ensuring you spend time doing things you enjoy will automatically lift your mood

10

Confidence Guaranteed

Here lies the secret to building confidence that lasts. Exciting, right? All you need to do is start working towards achievable goals within a framework of personal values and you'll feel better about yourself, your skills and your abilities.

Ambitions lists

Congratulations, you have reached the final stage in the battle against insecurity, which is no small feat. But don't worry, we're not going to pack you off without revealing the one final secret behind true and lasting confidence so, drum roll please …

The big fat secret behind lasting confidence

True confidence is a result of feeling happy and fulfilled both personally and professionally – discovering what gives your life meaning and then working towards achieving it.

That's it. It sounds so ridiculously simple, but it's scary how pootling along feeling a little lost – going through the motions – can become the norm. Feeling unfulfilled is the key to pretty much all confidence issues and so working towards something that you want to achieve will immediately make you feel good about yourself. Grabbing life by the neck and getting what you want out of it rather than watching it slip by, helplessly, will make you feel motivated, inspired, happy and hopeful. To feel truly confident you have to start thinking about what you want to do in your life and the values you want to live by. The best way of doing that is to make yourself an ambitions list.

An ambitions list is a slightly more interesting name for a plain old plan. Planning what you want to do in your life and how you're going to do it will quadruple your chances of actually doing it, rather than just thinking vaguely, 'oh yeah, I wouldn't mind trying that one day'. It will clarify the direction you want to head in, the things you want to focus on, and what's really important to you.

Going after a goal will make you feel proud for taking action and confident because you'll be able to prove to yourself that you can complete something successfully and you don't have to be frightened of the unknown. Goals provide a sense of purpose and hope, and are a great way of looking past the daily grind. Developing a bigger picture and creating and working towards meaningful and achievable goals will update how you define yourself. You're not the same person you were yesterday, you're someone with a clear aim. Lots of studies show people regret the things they didn't do much more than the things they did do.

Example: Joe's mind blank

Joe had been stuck in what he considered a dead-end job for years. There was no room for promotion and even though he'd tried to extend his role to include more challenging stuff, his managers stamped on any ingenuity through fear he'd want a pay rise or a different job title – neither of which they could give him.

His personal life was also a non-starter. A year ago he'd gone through a difficult break up and had been single since. He didn't know how to start dating again and he'd let some of his friendships slip and wasn't sure how to get them back on track. ⋯

⋯∴ Every day dragged and he felt like he had nothing to look forward to. All he really wanted to do was write a novel, but because he had no formal training and hadn't written so much as a postcard for several years, he felt unqualified and stupid for even thinking about it. He hadn't ever told anyone about this dream because he believed people would laugh at him. Other people wrote novels, not people like him. How dare he think about writing a book?!

By simply accepting that his desire to write is valid and worth considering, Joe would already feel better about it. At the moment he's hiding it like a guilty secret, as if it's something to be ashamed of. Everyone likes feeling safe and secure, but your comfort zone can become a cage, keeping you from stretching yourself and experiencing anything new. People are only ever rewarded when they strike out and challenge themselves, when they feel like they're learning and achieving. When things tick along as expected your brain won't even raise an eyebrow, but when you do something unexpected everything jumps into action – you'll feel excited and motivated, your body will become alert and your behaviour will reflect this new drive. It's important to seek out novelty in your life.

If Joe wrote down 'Aim: write a novel' in his notebook and then broke that aim down into manageable steps he'd feel a thrill of anticipation. The steps could be:

Joe's mind map looks like this:

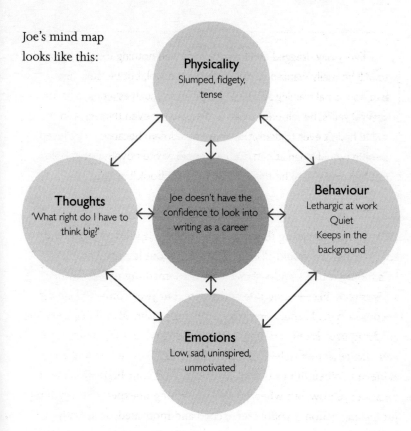

1 Look into creative writing classes
2 Phone up to enquire
3 Join a class
4 Ask the tutor for help in deciding the next step

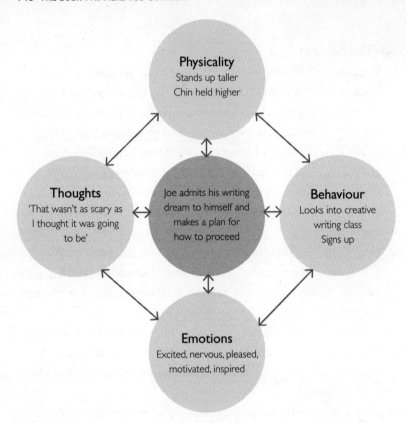

Making that list would change Joe's mind map to look more like the one above.

Having a plan focuses your mind, rather than seeing ideas as pipe dreams you start making them a reality. Everyone has dreams – why would anyone laugh at yours? You have to believe that these things are possible. No one became a novelist, a painter or an entrepreneur by sitting on their arse and waiting to be asked. You have to take steps to make it happen. And never forget: everyone has to start somewhere.

⑤ The big idea

1 Write down a list of anything that you haven't yet done in your life, but that you want to do. Nothing is too big or too small. It can be anything from 'change my hairstyle' to 'learn to fly a plane'. Consider countries you want to visit, that promotion you want to get, volunteering or having kids. Make sure you include both professional and personal goals, as well as ones that can involve family and friends. (Including other people will make you more likely to see the plan through.) Don't let cost implications get in the way at the moment.

2 Next, divide the list into short-term, medium-term and long-term goals and give each a timescale that's realistic for you, e.g. six months for short-term, 1–5 years for medium-term and 5–10 years for long-term.

3 Rank the goals in order of ease, i.e. put the ones that are affordable, practical and will take the least time at the top of your list and the ones that will take longer, could be expensive and time-consuming at the bottom.

4 Break down the bigger goals into manageable steps like Joe did with his novelist dream. Smaller steps will make it seem less overwhelming and will motivate you to actually get started. As you complete each section you'll gain in confidence, and feel more able and excited about tackling the next bit.

5 Don't dismiss seemingly impossible dreams. If you've written 'become a pilot', but you're blind in one eye and scared of heights break the idea down. What are the rules for flying? Could you look into tandem flights? Could you start small and get bigger? Is your

dream of piloting actually just a way for you to stop being scared of heights? Is that the goal you really want to meet? If so, could you look into phobia classes? You may have to compromise on some things, but actually finding ways around them will make you feel better than writing them off altogether.

6 And then ... start! Begin with the simple and easy tasks first. Seeing progress will encourage you to face the bigger long-term plans.

Remember: these goals should always be about what you can do. Don't focus on something that relies on other people because they have their own priorities and could let you down through no fault of their own. Involving other people is great, but only if the success of the task isn't dependent on them.

Try to do something towards your goals every single day as this will keep your focus, maintain momentum, and make working on them a habit so you'll be less tempted to file the list away under 'things to think about another day'.

Some people find it inspiring to keep a photo diary of their achievements. Whenever they tick something off the list they record it with a snap and a short note listing the date and time, what happened and how they felt. There's nothing as encouraging as looking back at past successes. There are also plenty of Twitter and Facebook feeds where people chat about their plans for the future and what they're working towards. Seeing other people's journeys can be really inspiring.

The point of this isn't to plough through the list, ticking everything off in a frenzy, it's to enjoy the journey. You need to savour what you're doing and how you're doing it. For example, if you're saving for a round-the-world trip reward yourself every time you put away another £250. Go out for a drink or keep your friend posted whenever you reach another goal. Celebrating your milestones is an easy way to feel good about what you're doing and to ensure you keep it up.

A personal valuation

Now you've sorted out what you're going to be working towards, you should also consider how you're going to work towards it. Guiding principles are values that you live your life by irrespective of changes in your circumstances. They will give you drive, fulfilment and integrity. Often we get so caught up in the minutiae of our lives, it's easy to forget the big things. Reassessing what you find important will remind you to channel those things into your day-to-day life.

⑤ Choosing your guiding principles

+ Pick out five values that you consider the most integral to your life and then rank them in order of importance on a scale of 1–5 (1 being the most important and 5 being the least).
+ Next, pick out the five values that are the least important to you and rank those in order too (with 1 being the least valuable).

Most important	Least important
1 Confidence	1 Authority
2 Fun	2 Popularity
3 Loyalty	3 Safety
4 Love	4 Power
5 Ambition	5 Virtue

This exercise is all about accepting what is important to you and then using those values to shape your life. They shouldn't be based on what you think others value or what your mate thinks is important. It's about what you think is important.

Whatever you decide you want to focus on just make sure you feel fulfilled. If your list of goals is all work-based and your most important values are 'ambition', 'wealth', 'success' and 'control', but you don't feel any better about yourself even when you're ticking things off your list, then it's time to reassess your values. Maybe you haven't defined success in a way that's right for you – it's not necessarily financial or professional, it's about feeling fulfilled in your personal life too. Choosing what you want to focus on will make you more aware of how you're living your life at the moment and what could be missing. It's never too late to change and to be who you want to be. These aren't definitive, please add some of your own if we've missed any.

Value list

Acceptance: to feel accepted among my peers

Achievement: to achieve what I set out to

Ambition: to always strive to better myself

Attractiveness: to look after my personal appearance

Caring: to always take other people's feelings and circumstances into consideration

Compassion: to feel concern for others and myself

Confidence: to have faith in my own skills and abilities

Courtesy: to be polite and considerate to others

Creativity: to have original ideas

Dependability: to be reliable and trustworthy

Fairness: to be fair to myself and to others

Family: to have a happy, loving family

Flexibility: to adjust to new or unusual situations easily

Friendliness: to have close and supportive friends and to be considered friendly to others

Fun: to be considered good company and to take time out to enjoy myself

Generosity: to give what I can to others

Health: to be physically well and healthy

Honesty: to be truthful and genuine – as far as possible!

Humility: to be modest and not unnecessarily self-promoting

Humour: to always try to see the funny side

Independence: to trust myself and my decision-making abilities

Justice: to make sure I promote equal and fair treatment to others whenever I can

Knowledge: to never stop learning

Love: to be loved by those close to me and to love others

Loyalty: to be considered reliable and trustworthy

Popularity: to be well liked by many people

Power: to have control over others

Realism: to see things realistically and in as objective a way as possible

Religion: to follow the teachings of my chosen religion

Respect: to have people respect, trust and look up to me and to respect, trust and look up to other people

Responsibility: to make and carry out important decisions to the best of my ability and knowledge

Risk: to take risks and make the most of opportunities that come my way

Safety: to be safe and secure in what I think and what I do

Self-control: to be disciplined and govern my own actions

Self-esteem: to like myself, just as I am

Self-knowledge: to have a deep, honest understanding of myself

Sexuality: to have an active and satisfying sex life

Spirituality: to grow spiritually

Strength: to be physically strong and/ or to nurture an inner strength

Success: to achieve everything I set out to, or at least give it a try

Tolerance: to accept and respect those different from me

Virtue: to live a good – a moral – life

Wealth: to have plenty of money

Thoughts to take away

✓ Making goals will give your life meaning and make you feel fulfilled

✓ Working towards something you really want to achieve will build your confidence

✓ Acknowledging the values that are important to you will motivate you to be the person you want to be

A final message

Congratulations! You've made it to the end of the book hopefully feeling more confident, secure and happy in yourself than you did before you started. We're crossing all our fingers and toes that you're now thinking about yourself in a much more realistic and balanced way.

Confidence is about giving yourself credit where it's due and celebrating your strengths and successes – however it's also something that you have to learn. Changing your beliefs about yourself is an on-going process that will take time. It took a while to build up the negative view you had of yourself, so it'll take time to break it down. All of which means that if you're not dancing a merry jig about how amazing you are yet, don't panic. Building confidence takes practice. You need to re-train your attention to stop picking on the negatives and to start focusing on the things you do in a fair and consistent way. But if you feel even a tiny bit better about yourself and are looking forward to the future then throw yourself a party, because that's brilliant. Making these changes will have been – and will continue to be – hard work and recognising how far you've come and what you've achieved is hugely important.

As a means to measure how far you've come please answer the below questions:

1 **After reading the book – how do you feel?**

   A The same – no change

   B A smidgen better – starting to think this all through

   C Better – putting in place improvements

   D Amazing - transformed

If you answered option A did you really invest all your energy into the strategies? Are you willing to try them again? If you are still having difficulties and the book hasn't helped you as much as you'd hoped, then we suggest speaking to your GP who should be able to recommend further treatment. There are some useful resources and websites at the back of the book.

If you answered B–D then we're very chuffed for you and things can only get better from here if you keep putting what you've learned into practice.

2 **Which of the 'takeaways' listed at the end of the chapters particularly struck a chord?** Write them down on a notepad or in your diary so every time you need a pick-me-up you can flick through and motivate yourself.

3 **What support network do you have to help you maintain what you've learned?** Consider telling family and friends what you're doing if you haven't already. Their encouragement will be invaluable and motivational – and talking things through can give you some clarity or a different perspective. It might also show you the funny side of a situation. Laughing at yourself and the situation will immediately lift your mood and make you feel lighter, happier and more able to cope.

4 **What possible obstacles do you see in the future that might throw you off course?** Write them down and then work through any solutions.

5 **Go back through the check list in Chapter 2 and tick the boxes that apply to you now.** How does the list compare to the one you did originally? Hopefully there will be a lot fewer boxes ticked! If

you have marked anything go through the book again to the relevant chapters and re-work the strategies until you feel confident you can beat them.

6 Are you going to stop NATs in their tracks and start being more realistic about yourself and the situations you find yourself in?

7 Are you going to stop making anxious doom-and-gloom predictions about everything and instead start taking risks?

8 Are you going to stand up tall, keep your head held high and generally try to look like someone who knows their own mind?

9 Are you going to make a list of short- medium- and long-term goals and start working towards them?

10 When are you going to start thinking differently?

   A I already have

   B Today

   C Tomorrow

   D Next week

   E Next year

   F I don't care

There are no right or wrong answers to these questions. This is a chance to assess how you feel now and if there are any specific areas you want to concentrate on. You now have the tools to feel more confident and to boost your self-esteem – how you use them is up to you. A fundamental message of this book is realising that you have choices. If you're excited about making changes then we salute you. It's really hard, but very rewarding. And it works.

If there are some bits of the book that you haven't tackled yet, go back and try again, reminding yourself what you're meant to be doing and why. It's incredibly difficult to change your behaviour and the way you think, especially when habits will have been built up over many years. However, it is possible. Often just considering doing things differently is the hardest bit – and you're well past that stage by now. Don't put undue pressure on yourself to change overnight. These things take time, but it's time well spent. Make a date to re-read the book in a month, six months or a year's time to see how differently you feel then and to keep the ideas fresh in your mind. And keep flicking through your notebook. It'll be really motivating to see how far you've come and to remind yourself of the tips and tricks that helped before.

Insecurity and low self-esteem can weigh on you and affect, detrimentally, your perception of life. But it doesn't have to be that way. You control what you do and how you do it. There will be times when you question yourself again – it's normal – but you now have the skills to navigate these blips, so you'll always know you can cope. Don't let life pass you by while you try to make up your mind whether or not to live it.

Confidence and self-esteem are essential to living a fulfilling and happy life and you deserve them both!

Further reading

Melanie Fennell, *Overcoming Low Self-Esteem* (London, Constable & Robinson, 2009)

Gillian Butler, *Overcoming Social Anxiety and Shyness* (London, Constable & Robinson, 2008)

Dennis Greenberg and Christine Padesky, *Mind over Mood: A Cognitive Treatment Manual for Clients* (New York, Guilford Press, 1995)

Useful websites

MIND, The National Association for Mental Health: www.mind.org.uk

Time to Change: www.time-to-change.org.uk

Mind Tools, Building Self Confidence: www.mindtools.com/selfconf.html

Social Anxiety UK: www.social-anxiety.org.uk

Moodjuice: www.moodjuice.scot.nhs.uk/shynesssocialphobia.asp

Be Mindful: bemindful.co.uk

Mood Gym: moodgym.anu.edu.au

Living Life to the Full: www.llttf.com

The Centre for Clinical Interventions: www.cci.health.wa.gov.au/resources

The Mental Health Foundation: www.mentalhealth.org.uk

The American Mental Health Foundation: americanmentalhealthfoundation.org

The Beck Institute: www.beckinstitute.org

Cruse Bereavement Care: www.cruse.org.uk

Relate: www.relate.org.uk/home/index.html

Frank: friendly confidential drugs advice: www.talktofrank.com

Alcohol Concern: www.alcoholconcern.org.uk

The British Psychological Society: www.bps.org.uk

The British Association for Behavioural & Cognitive Psychotherapy: www.babcp.com

Samaritans: www.samaritans.org

Acknowledgements

Thanks to all the people who believed in these books and helped to make them happen. Big thanks to our wonderful families, particularly Ben, Jack, Max and Edie. Also to our agent Jane Graham Maw for brilliant advice, our editor Kerry Enzor for her contagious enthusiasm and Peggy Sadler for her unsurpassed design skills. Jessamy would also like to thank the psychologists, health professionals and patients who have educated, supported and inspired her.